—— A New ——

Division of Labor

Meeting America's Security Challenges Beyond Iraq

Andrew R. Hoehn, Adam Grissom, David A. Ochmanek
David A. Shlapak, Alan J. Vick

Prepared for the United States Air Force

Approved for public release; distribution unlimited

PROJECT AIR FORCE

The research described in this report was sponsored by the United States Air Force under Contract F49642-01-C-0003. Further information may be obtained from the Strategic Planning Division, Directorate of Plans, Hq USAF.

Library of Congress Cataloging-in-Publication Data

A new division of labor : meeting America's security challenges beyond Iraq / Andrew R. Hoehn ... [et al.].
    p. cm.
    RAND Project Air Force.
    Includes bibliographical references.
    ISBN 978-0-8330-3962-0 (pbk. : alk. paper)
    1. United States—Military policy. 2. United States—Armed Forces—Reorganization. 3. World politics—21st century. I. Hoehn, Andrew R.

UA23.N375 2007
355'.033573—dc22

                                                                    2006102730

The RAND Corporation is a nonprofit research organization providing objective analysis and effective solutions that address the challenges facing the public and private sectors around the world. RAND's publications do not necessarily reflect the opinions of its research clients and sponsors.

RAND® is a registered trademark.

Cover design by Stephen Bloodsworth

Published 2007 by the RAND Corporation
1776 Main Street, P.O. Box 2138, Santa Monica, CA 90407-2138
1200 South Hayes Street, Arlington, VA 22202-5050
4570 Fifth Avenue, Suite 600, Pittsburgh, PA 15213-2665
RAND URL: http://www.rand.org/
To order RAND documents or to obtain additional information, contact
Distribution Services: Telephone: (310) 451-7002;
Fax: (310) 451-6915; Email: order@rand.org

Preface

In January 2005, George W. Bush committed the nation to the extraordinary goal of "ending tyranny in our world," a goal consistent with Bush's earlier national security statements but one that had not been expressed before in such expansive fashion.

Since then, there has been a storm of debate in the United States and abroad about the appropriateness of this goal as a motivating factor for U.S. foreign policy. To the extent that Americans equate "ending tyranny" with toppling hostile regimes, as in Iraq, and replacing them with new forms of representative government, they are divided on the issue and increasingly suspicious of the prospects for success. But to the extent that Americans see "ending tyranny" as a broader, long-term response to the challenges posed by terrorism rooted in radical interpretations of Islam and the proliferation of destructive technology, a consensus appears to be emerging that this is an appropriate strategy for the United States and its allies. Should this broader strategy be sustained, as we expect it will, this will have far-reaching effects on the institutions of the U.S. government.

This monograph explores the implications of this strategy and of key factors shaping the international security environment for the Department of Defense (DoD). We focused on DoD for two key reasons:

- First, the armed forces of the United States have been used to spearhead this new strategy, and they have achieved important successes. But it is also clear that, in several instances, U.S. armed forces are being called on to perform missions that are well outside their normal repertoire. If these missions are only temporary, ad hoc arrangements may suffice. But if these new missions represent a more permanent set of demands on the armed forces, pursuant to an enduring change in strategy, more lasting changes need to be considered.

- Second, and on a more urgent basis, DoD is again involved in a major review of strategy and policy, which follows on the recent Quadrennial Defense Review. This review and the period of implementation that will follow it offer the administration the opportunity to consider anew the demands of the international security environment, missions assigned to the armed forces, proper emphasis among these missions, and allocation of resources allotted to them.

The purpose of this effort is to offer ideas and insights to the leadership of DoD on key issues as it strives to align defense resources and capabilities with the demands of a new strategy and stressing security environment.

The approach taken in this monograph aims first and foremost to explore the implications of a new and demanding strategy. Examining threats to the objectives embodied in that strategy, we define what would logically be the central elements of a defense strategy appropriate to the conditions likely to emerge in the coming years. Forces and posture are then examined to determine how well they provide the capabilities most appropriate to implementing that strategy.

The work presented here does not seek to address important issues relating to broader institutions of government, which should be the subject of a separate study, or the management of DoD, including acquisition reform, the industrial base, business and accounting practices, or personnel management. Neither does this monograph attempt in any direct way to address the question of whether the aggregate level of resources the United States is devoting to its armed forces is appropriate, although this work recognizes that resource constraints are significant today and are likely to tighten in the years ahead.

Finally, although the recommendations put forward in this report are based on the authors' judgments regarding future strategy and the implementation of that strategy, many of the same recommendations could be made with the objective of achieving greater efficiency within DoD.

We have drawn on work undertaken at the RAND Corporation and elsewhere over the past several years. Chief among our sources have been assessments of international terrorism and strategies for defeating terrorist groups; war games featuring hostile regional powers armed with nuclear weapons and the means to deliver them; operational analyses of possible scenarios involving conflict over Taiwan; detailed evaluations of concepts and systems for airborne and space-based surveillance; assessments of evolving threats to airfields and other key components of military infrastructure in potential theaters of conflict; and, importantly, lessons from recent wars.

Although it is not practicable to provide the full rationale behind the many judgments and recommendations contained in the monograph, substantial amounts of research and analysis underlie our findings and much of the documentation of this work is available to the public.[1]

RAND Project AIR FORCE

RAND Project AIR FORCE (PAF), a division of the RAND Corporation, is the U.S. Air Force's federally funded research and development center for studies and analyses. PAF provides the Air Force with independent analyses of policy alternatives affecting the development, employment, combat readiness, and support of current and future aerospace forces. Research is conducted in four programs: Aerospace Force Development; Manpower, Personnel, and Training; Resource Management; and Strategy and Doctrine. Integrative research projects and work on modeling and simulation are conducted on a PAF-wide

---

[1] Publicly available sources relevant to the material presented in this monograph are cited in the bibliography. Several of these sources and others are available through the RAND Web site: http://www.rand.org.

basis. The research reported here was prepared within the Strategy and Doctrine program.

Additional information about PAF is available on our Web site at http://www.rand.org/paf.

Contents

Summary

In January 2005, George W. Bush took the oath of office for his second term as President. In his inaugural address, Bush pledged his administration to "seek and support the growth of democratic movements in every nation and culture, with the ultimate goal of ending tyranny in the world." In so doing, he echoed a widely held sentiment that, over the long run, safeguarding America against extremism and tyranny will require a national commitment to fostering democracy, stability, and prosperity in other societies.

In a sense, this is a natural, almost reflexive American response to a threat to core U.S. interests. The spread of democracy and freedom has been a prominent feature of American policy and culture since the founding of the republic. It had been a key theme of nearly every 20th-century president and, in fact, animated Wilson and Roosevelt as they sought to shape the outcomes of the two great wars of that century. Moreover, it was a theme that motivated Bush's immediate predecessors, particularly William Clinton, and led to American support for emerging democracies in Latin America, East Asia, and South Africa, as well as American military involvement in such places as the Balkans.

But, in another sense, it represents a sharp departure for American foreign and security policy in that this administration has demonstrated a willingness not only to stand up to America's foes but also discomfit its friends. In pursuit of this strategy since September 11, 2001, the United States has demonstrated a willingness, in some cases, to create near-term instability to secure longer-term goals.

This expansive strategy has important implications for the entire national security establishment, and diplomats and soldiers alike are adapting to new demands and seeking to define new roles. Should the nation continue to pursue the broad contours of this strategy, if not some of the specific applications—and we believe that there is every evidence that it will[2]—the institutions of government will, of necessity, change and adapt, much as they did when America accepted new global responsibilities at the end of World War II.

A New Grand Strategy?

Just as in the late 1940s, when it took the emergence of a clear and compelling threat—Soviet expansionism backed by powerful military forces—to induce the United States to shake off its tradition of isolationism and adopt the strategy of containment, so too did the shock of 9/11 prompt this nation to put forth a far-reaching and ambitious national security strategy. That strategy, the centerpiece of which is promoting democracy and freedom abroad, is the necessary response to conditions that can breed serious threats to the security of Americans worldwide. Although this strategy has roots in all post–Cold War administrations, it has been given clearest expression by the current administration in the wake of 9/11. As a consensus forms around the idea that the United States and its allies must work to extend the reach of democracy and freedom, this strategy could come to be recognized as the long-awaited replacement for containment. (See pp. 3–7.)

The strategy is nothing if not ambitious. Pursuing this strategy in earnest will require the United States and its partners to marshal substantial levels of resources and to apply them with patience and commitment. It will require the energy of the public and private sectors and a renewed focus on diplomacy, education, outreach, and assis-

---

[2]   In judging that the nation will continue on this path for the foreseeable future, we also recognize that different leaders will interpret this strategy in different ways. Just as "containment" was modified and adapted over the long years of the Cold War, so too will the strategy to promote democracy and freedom take different forms.

tance. It will also call for the involvement of, and significant changes to, America's armed forces.

Conflict in the Post Post–Cold War World

A new and expansive strategy, along with challenges posed by adversaries of the United States and its allies, will place daunting demands on America's military forces. Three in particular present novel and stern challenges to the armed forces of the United States:

- **Terrorist and insurgent groups.** Poverty, weak governance, and conflicts over identity have helped to create conditions that terrorists and insurgents can exploit. The spread of technological know-how related to means of killing—ranging from powerful explosive devices to biological and, ultimately, nuclear weapons—is giving small groups the means to kill thousands. By harnessing militant interpretations of Islam to new means of violence, al Qaeda and related groups have created a virulent threat that all responsible states must act to defeat. (See pp. 14–15.)
- **Regional powers with nuclear weapons.** Such states as North Korea and Iran appear determined to acquire nuclear weapons. Indeed, it is possible that North Korea already possesses a limited number of nuclear weapons. They and others, including terrorist organizations, have access to a worldwide supply chain that is not entirely under the control of states. If such adversaries succeed in fielding deliverable nuclear weapons, the implications for regional stability and the security of U.S. allies will be highly troubling. In the short run, the U.S. armed forces will face a challenge in posturing themselves appropriately for such contingencies in a way that reassures U.S. allies of its commitment to their security. In the long run, the challenge for this and future administrations will be coupling the appropriate military posture with a long-term political framework for evolving these societies toward democracy, stability, and integration into regional security structures. (See pp. 16–19.)

- **Military competition in Asia.** Arguably, U.S. forces can prevail over the conventional forces of any nation, provided the full panoply of U.S. capabilities can be brought to bear. Recognizing this, regional adversaries are focusing their military investments on capabilities that can be used to impede U.S. forces from getting to the fight. China, with its burgeoning economy and growing technological sophistication, is fielding the most impressive set of such capabilities. They include advanced air defenses; numerous systems for attacking surface ships; antisatellite weapons; and, most troublingly, large numbers of accurate, long-range strike systems, principally conventionally armed ballistic and cruise missiles. These weapons not only can keep U.S. expeditionary forces at bay for significant periods but also be used to coerce and intimidate the leadership of Taiwan and other states in the region. The challenge here, again, will be coupling an appropriate military posture vis-à-vis China with a long-term effort to integrate it into the international system as a stable, responsible power. (See pp. 19–24.)

Meeting These Challenges

These developments carry several implications for U.S. defense planners:

- First, a substantial and sustained level of effort to suppress terrorist and insurgent groups abroad is essential if the nation is to make headway against the threats they pose.[3] For DoD, this will sometimes take the form of direct action to locate and capture or kill terrorists and insurgents. Far more often, it will involve undertaking indirect actions, principally long-term, "hands-on" efforts to train, equip, advise, and assist the forces of nations that seek to suppress these groups in their own territories. (See pp 28–31.)

---

[3] We recognize that not all fragile states will invite terrorists and that not all terrorist struggles are insurgencies in character.

- Related to this, U.S. forces will be called on to help bring stability and security to nations struggling to implement democratic reforms. This will involve providing support to defeat internal threats and shoring up regional security to cope with external enemies. (See pp. 31–33.)
- To sustain deterrence against hostile regional states and, in the future, to counter nonstate adversaries, U.S. forces must develop and field far more effective means for locating and destroying or otherwise defending against nuclear weapons and their means of delivery. (See pp. 33–35.)
- U.S. forces must also ensure that they can overcome modern anti-access weapons and methods. Of particular urgency is the need for highly effective, wide-area defenses against theater ballistic missiles. Cruise missiles also are a concern. (See pp. 36–38.)

America's new strategy, combined with daunting challenges emanating from states and nonstate adversaries, will impose new demands on U.S. armed forces. These demands will stress our forces both qualitatively (by creating needs for new types of capabilities) and quantitatively (calling for high and sustained levels of commitment abroad). At the same time, fiscal realities are placing strict limits on the resources available not only for defense but also for important related activities, such as counterproliferation initiatives, international development assistance, and public diplomacy. This combination of an ambitious strategy, a dynamic and challenging threat environment, and tightly constrained resources creates a profound dilemma for military strategists and force planners. How might these factors be reconciled?

Recasting U.S. Defense Strategy

DoD first needs to define a defense strategy that embraces the goal of extending the reach of democracy and freedom. This will not, in our estimation, necessarily involve more instances of forcible regime change along the lines of Operation Iraqi Freedom. Rather, it means placing far more emphasis than heretofore on helping to create or enhance stability in key areas abroad so that governments can effectively control their own territories. We refer to this as *stability operations*, by which we mean both direct counterinsurgency and other irregular operations by U.S. forces and, more importantly and more often, indirect efforts to train, equip, and advise allied indigenous forces. Practically speaking, this means that the force sizing criterion posited by the defense strategy of 2001—"1-4-2-1"—should be recast.[4] Specifically, the nation will no longer be able to limit its day-to-day activities and posture to only the four regions in which it is deemed to have important geopolitical interests, as classically defined: Europe, Northeast Asia, the East Asian littoral, and the Middle East and Southwest Asia. It is now clear that such seemingly remote areas as Afghanistan, Sudan, the Horn of Africa, the Sahel, Central Asia, the Philippines, and Indonesia can gestate serious threats not only to regional peace and stability but also to American security interests. In fact, the number of places in which U.S. and allied forces might be called on to engage in promoting stability, democracy, and military competence is indeterminate. Thus, in our assessment, "4" has, of necessity, become "n."[5]

At the same time, the familiar missions of deterring aggression, redressing imbalances in military power, and defeating aggression through large-scale power-projection operations have not diminished in importance. In fact, these missions are, in many ways, becoming more challenging. Protecting U.S. national interests in Southwest Asia, East Asia, and elsewhere will demand that U.S. forces, in conjunction

---

[4] The criterion that became known as "1-4-2-1" directed the armed forces to be prepared simultaneously to defend the United States (1), deter aggression and coercion in four critical regions (4), and swiftly defeat aggression in two overlapping conflicts (2), while preserving the option to impose a change of regime in one of the conflicts (1). It also stated that the forces were to be able to conduct a limited number of smaller-scale contingency operations. For further elaboration, see DoD (2001).

[5] DoD, in its 2006 *Quadrennial Defense Review Report*, has recognized this, stating that U.S. forces must be structured and postured to operate on a sustained basis "around the globe and not only in and from the four regions called out in the 2001 QDR" (see DoD, 2006, p. 36). DoD has not, however, indicated how forces should be configured for these operations or where the capacity to sustain them will come from. For purposes of force planning, DoD should designate a rotation base of forces capable of sustaining roughly 50 "train, equip, and advise" missions of various size and duration worldwide (see Chapter Five).

with those of our allies, remain able to defeat the forces of adversary states in more than one region. This is critically important not only to credibly deter our adversaries but also to assure our allies and partners. Needless to say, U.S. forces must also do whatever is necessary to protect the United States itself. (See pp. 41–45.)

The question then becomes whether and how DoD can support a demanding "1-n-2-1" criterion for sizing and shaping the armed forces of the United States.

A New Division of Labor

The first thing to recognize is that the demands of "1-n-2-1" need not apply equally to every branch of the armed forces. The imperative to promote stability and democracy abroad will place the greatest demands on America's ground forces—the Army and the Marine Corps—and special operations forces (SOF). Air and naval forces can make important contributions to these missions, principally in the areas of intelligence, lift, base operating support or offshore bases, and humanitarian support. But by and large, these missions call for substantial commitments of ground forces to work directly with their host-country counterparts. By the same token, the most plausible major combat operations that U.S. forces might be called on to fight in the coming years—involving Iran, China (over Taiwan), and North Korea—call for heavy commitments of air and naval forces and, in the first two cases, smaller numbers of U.S. ground forces.

Given limited resources, including limited numbers of available personnel, the nation's leaders face a choice of where to apportion risk: Either they can continue to ask U.S. ground forces to prepare for major wars and risk a diminished ability to operate effectively in direct and indirect stability operations, or they can focus a much larger proportion of U.S. ground forces on such missions and accept the risk of shifting some of the burden for large force-on-force contingencies to air and naval forces. Given the demands of America's new strategy, the certainty of the need for a sustained level of effort against terrorist and insurgent groups, and recent advances in the ability to use pre-

cision firepower to shape the battlefield to the ground commander's
advantage, we suggest that DoD's leaders consider the latter course.
Such a decision would permit the Army and Marine Corps, in conjunction with SOF, to improve their stability operations capabilities
qualitatively and quantitatively by relieving these two services of the
requirement to provide forces for more than one major war. Taking
this step would help keep overall demands on the forces of these two
services manageable. Equally important, it would also permit substantial portions of both services to optimize training, doctrine, and equipment on the development of forces for manpower-intensive operations
now demanded by America's new strategy. Under this construct, the
Navy and Air Force would retain their primary focus on large-scale
power-projection operations, although both services will be called on
to provide essential enabling capabilities for direct and indirect stability operations. Both will also need to place much greater emphasis on
defeating enemies armed with nuclear weapons and with more sophisticated antiaccess capabilities than have heretofore been encountered.
(See pp. 45–47.)

Potential Actions

The foregoing considerations suggest that DoD's leaders should consider the following actions to bring America's defense capabilities into
better alignment with the nation's new strategy:

- **Recast U.S. defense strategy to incorporate "1-n-2-1" as its force
  sizing construct.** Relieve the Army and Marine Corps of the
  requirement to provide forces for more than one major combat
  operation at a time. Bringing stability to troubled nations, training and advising the forces of other countries, and conducting
  effective operations against insurgents and terrorists are important, complex, and politically charged missions. A greater level
  of effort is called for here if we and our allies are to make lasting progress against global terrorist threats. The accumulation of
  recent experience suggests that these missions cannot be done well

by forces whose primary focus is large-scale combat. Changes in the nature of the threats regional adversaries pose will allow DoD to reduce the level of ground forces it plans to commit to major combat operations. (See pp. 40–45.)

- **Complete the transition of the joint command structure.** Regional commanders need to remain focused on strategic matters, including achieving strategic victory in areas where U.S. forces are engaged. To allow them to do so, more, and more effective, joint task force headquarters are needed for running ongoing operations. Ongoing efforts in this regard at U.S. Joint Forces Command should be buttressed. Moreover, the joint division of labor among regional commands, global commands, and military services and supporting agencies should be clarified. The concept of a division of labor among users, managers, and providers may be useful in guiding this effort. (See pp. 52–55.)
- **Complete the effort to realign U.S. global military posture; reevaluate that posture regularly.** The overseas posture of U.S. military forces and bases should directly reflect broader U.S. strategy. That is not the case today. Forces and facilities will need to be realigned to support new democracies, counter terrorist and insurgent groups, deter and defeat regional adversaries, and dissuade military competition in Asia. Current plans for adjusting the global basing structure should be implemented and reevaluated regularly to ensure that U.S. strategy and posture remain in proper alignment. (See pp. 47–50.)
- **Increase investments in promising systems for surveillance and reconnaissance.** U.S. defense planners should aspire to put an end to the situation in which sensor systems and the means to interpret the information they acquire are chronically "low-density, high-demand" assets. And efforts should be made to accelerate the development of new systems better suited to finding such targets as mobile missiles, nuclear weapons, and small groups of armed combatants. (See pp. 61–64.)

But realigning the defense strategy and reallocating risk alone will not provide the needed results. New partnerships need to be formed (and old ones need to be strengthened); new capabilities need to be developed; and new competencies need to be cultivated. These include the following:

- **Foster new and stronger partnerships among the military services to achieve greater strategic and operational depth and joint tactical proficiency.** Even as diversification among military services and agencies is required to support U.S. strategy, new interdependencies need to be forged. We view this as something akin to brokering a new set of partnerships among the military services. The process will be difficult, but in our judgment it is essential. (See pp. 55–57.)

  – **Partnership 1: Develop and implement plans for air and land forces to train for and to conduct highly integrated operations.** To become more strategically deployable and agile on the battlefield, the Army is reducing its organic artillery and increasingly relying on air-delivered fires. Recent operations have demonstrated the potential of this concept, but it is far from established as a new way of war. Realistic air-ground exercises and training are rare, and procedures for controlling and integrating air operations and ground maneuver are outdated. The services need to see themselves as mutually enabling partners. Regular joint training, new fire-control mechanisms (including investments in new gear for tactical air controllers), and cultural changes will be necessary to realize the potential of the air-ground partnership. (See pp. 76–80.)

  – **Partnership 2: Foster much tighter links among air, naval, and space forces to create a more-durable, more-effective power-projection force.** Without better integrating the capabilities of America's air, naval, and space forces, the U.S. military runs the risk of not having an effective power-projection capability against adversaries with ballistic and cruise missiles, advanced air defenses, and perhaps nuclear weapons. Forging robust links will require more routine training and the development of common command-and-control procedures and mechanisms. (See pp. 80–88.)

- **Partnership 3: Promote a more-seamless integration between the Marine Corps and SOF.** Just as the Marine Corps could give SOF more depth by providing combined-arms support for sensitive SOF missions, so too could the Marine Corps give SOF more reach by expanding the area and frequency of routine SOF missions and activities. These two branches have much in common, and they should exploit the exceptional qualities of both. This implies less focus on the Marine Corps' traditional amphibious missions and much more openness in the SOF community to cooperating with another military branch. (See pp. 89–92.)

- **Pursue an aggressive effort to develop and produce more-effective defenses against theater ballistic missiles and cruise missiles.** These weapons, whether armed with accurate conventional warheads or nuclear weapons, pose grave obstacles to U.S. power-projection operations. Indeed, for the first time since the conclusion of the Cold War, the United States faces the prospect that its forces could be defeated or excluded from the fight. Large concentrations of troops and materiel within range of enemy missiles will be at great risk. And it may prove impossible to mount effective combat operations from even hardened fixed bases within range of these weapons. Because of the importance of protecting the civilian populations and infrastructures of allied nations, special emphasis should be placed on developing concepts for layered theater missile defenses that are effective over wide areas. Truly effective defenses will require the fielding of larger numbers of existing theater missile defense systems (e.g., the Theater High-Altitude Area Defense and the Navy's SM-3) and one or more additional "layers" of active defense. (See pp. 83–85.)

- **Greatly expand the capacity and competence of forces devoted to combat advisory and training missions.** New democracies and friendly nations threatened by insurgent and terrorist groups will look to the United States for assistance. It is neither desirable nor feasible to send U.S. ground forces routinely to fight other countries' insurgencies. Rather, the most effective means for DoD to counter terrorist and insurgent groups abroad is to train, equip,

xx A New Division of Labor

advise, and assist the forces of friendly governments. The United States already possesses first-rate combat advisors and trainers in all the services, but their numbers are small, resources are limited, and activities are greatly restricted. Substantial portions of the "regular" forces must contribute to this vital mission. Although the largest number of advisors will likely come from the Army and Marine Corps, the advisory capabilities of the Navy and Air Force need to expand as well. Expanded foreign area officer programs in the services are essential to develop the language and cultural understanding necessary to be effective advisors. (See pp. 68–73, 86–87, 92–96.)

Finally, specific entities within DoD will need to adopt different approaches, develop new or refined capabilities, and cultivate new talents. But these changes will likely need outside intervention to "jump start" the activity. We have highlighted the most important of these changes, including the following:

- **Direct the Army to explore creating distinct elements within its tactical structure. One element would specialize in conventional warfighting operations, and the other would specialize in stability, support, and advisory operations.** Resource constraints and limitations on the ability of soldiers to master and maintain widely divergent skill sets make it impossible for the Army to fully prepare its entire tactical structure for both conventional warfighting and stability operations. By bifurcating its tactical structure, the Army would free the units assigned conventional missions to prepare more fully for warfighting operations and would free the units assigned to stability operations to prepare more fully for these difficult missions. The result would be that the Army as a whole would become more proficient at both. (See pp. 68–71.)
- **Direct the Army to create doctrine and a professional military education curriculum that emphasize stability operations.** Current doctrine and curriculum focus on conventional warfighting to the near exclusion of stability operations. This imbalance should be corrected by balancing capstone and operational-level

doctrine equally between warfighting and stability operations. Tactical doctrine and training literature will likely need to be bifurcated by mission as well. (See pp. 73–75.)

- **Direct the Air Force to reevaluate its concepts for large-scale power-projection operations, assessing in particular the implications for its mix of long- and short-range platforms.** The Air Force's planned investments in new combat aircraft implicitly reflect the belief that forces will be able to deploy forward and conduct high-tempo operations from air bases in the theater of conflict. Such assumptions seem increasingly untenable. A platform mix that increases emphasis on long-range platforms for surveillance and strike would provide commanders more options for basing aircraft in locales less threatened by attack from enemy missiles. It would also provide more "battle space," allowing defensive systems more opportunities to engage incoming missiles. Longer-range platforms would also be better suited to providing enduring, responsive information and fire support to joint forces on battlefields where enemy forces are less likely to be massed and more likely to be encountered episodically. (See pp. 85–88.)

- **Help rebuild the nation's intelligence system—and, by implication, DoD's intelligence capabilities—by focusing first and foremost on the human dimension.** New sensors, platforms, and technologies are vital to answering the challenges of the future security environment—and we believe that a thorough reassessment of investment priorities is needed. However, above all, enabling decisionmakers at the tactical, operational, and strategic levels demands properly trained and experienced people throughout the collection, assessment, and dissemination chain. Especially within the four military services, more people are needed with the skills to understand the political and social dynamics in troubled regions. And institutional incentives must be put in place to create satisfying career paths that encourage and reward professionalism. (See pp. 61–64.)

- **Direct U.S. air forces to train more frequently with SOF and the ground forces of friendly nations.** In most cases, U.S. involvement in counterinsurgency operations will be limited to advising, equipping, and training. Where the threat is particularly great or host-nation capabilities are limited, the U.S. may want to provide direct operational support. Because a large or highly visible presence can undermine the credibility of the government the United States seeks to support, direct support must have a minimal footprint. U.S. air forces can provide critical surveillance, strike, and lift support in low-key ways, flying from remote bases or even from outside the assisted country. When combined with competent local ground forces, U.S. air forces can be extremely effective against insurgents. To be effective working with local forces, selected elements from U.S. air forces will need to train with U.S. SOF, U.S. Air Force terminal attack controllers, and allied ground forces on a regular basis. (See pp. 88–89.)

Finally, while striving to fix what is broken, DoD should be careful not to break what is fixed. The U.S. armed forces are the most powerful and successful in the world, perhaps in history. Their dominance of the conventional "force on force" battlefield is so overwhelming that it has, among other things, rendered a whole class of historically troubling scenarios—massed cross-border aggression by large, armored forces—largely obsolete. Maintaining appropriate levels of the capabilities that created this situation is critically important. Continued, selective investment in the areas in which the United States currently enjoys "overmatch" will be needed alongside the new initiatives required to address the nation's emerging security problems.

Acknowledgments

This monograph began as a series of detailed discussions at RAND in late winter 2005 and continued through 2006. What arose from these discussions was a growing conviction among the authors that the responsibilities being levied on U.S. armed forces had become so numerous and the tasks assigned to them so complex that multiple components of the defense establishment, including command arrangements, overseas posture, key programs, training regimes, and the defense strategy itself, needed to change. This volume is one result of these interactions. Its purpose is to draw together and integrate insights derived from a wide range of research efforts undertaken at RAND over the past few years.

The authors are especially grateful to Natalie Crawford, then–Vice President of RAND Project AIR FORCE, who reviewed the manuscript closely, offered numerous suggestions for improvement, and helped expedite the draft through the publication process. Two colleagues, Kevin Lewis of RAND and Gordon Adams of The George Washington University, provided formal reviews of the draft. Both were invaluable in pointing out needed clarifications and elaborations in the analysis and we are grateful to them for their expert advice. Bruce Bennett, Michael Decker, James Dobbins, Clark Murdock, James Thomson, and Joseph Wood also provided valuable comments and recommendations, as did numerous other officials and military leaders within the Department of Defense. The contributions of Colleen O'Connor and Sarah Harting were especially noteworthy: They managed the schedules and inputs of the contributors and ensured that the materials we developed were coherent and complete. Phyllis Gilmore edited the text, improving its clarity and precision throughout.

Abbreviations

DHL	Dalsey, Hillom, and Lynn (a transportation company)
DoD	Department of Defense
FCS	Future Combat System
FM	field manual
FY	fiscal year
GTEP	Georgia Train and Equip Program
ISR	intelligence, surveillance, and reconnaissance
JTF	joint task force
LHA	landing helicopter, assault (designates a general-purpose Navy amphibious assault ship)
LHD	landing helicopter deck (designates a general-purpose Navy amphibious assault ship)
MEU	Marine expeditionary unit
NATO	North Atlantic Treaty Organization
PAF	Project AIR FORCE
PLA	People's Liberation Army
QDR	Quadrennial Defense Review
SAM	surface-to-air missile

SEAL	sea-air-land team
SOF	special operations forces
TBM	theater ballistic missile
TMD	theater missile defense
TTP	tactics, techniques, and procedures
UAV	unmanned aircraft system
USS	United States ship
USJFCOM	U.S. Joint Forces Command
USSOCOM	U.S. Special Operations Command

CHAPTER ONE

Promoting Democracy and Freedom Abroad

The sudden collapse of the Soviet Union set off a debate in this country—and indeed throughout much of the world—on what should be the successor strategy to the long years of containment. With the threat of communist expansion no longer the central preoccupation of U.S. foreign and defense policy, a wide array of informed commentators considered fundamental questions regarding America's future role in the world. Their conclusions ranged from calls for a "new isolationism" to declarations of a "unipolar moment," with many variations in between.[1] Some focused on America's economic leadership in the world; others talked of America's responsibility to support and defend democracy abroad. Almost all who were involved in the debate wondered how the United States would redefine its leadership role in the world and how the world would respond to America's new pursuits.

Looking back over the last 15 years, it appears that the United States has indeed adopted a new approach to the world, that this approach is ambitious, and that a central focus of America's leadership will be on supporting and defending the emergence of freedom and democracy abroad. If America's role in the Cold War was to lead in the "defense of freedom,"[2] its goal in this new era is to expand the reach

---

[1] For a sampling of this debate, see Hyland (1990), Sorensen (1990), Nitze (1990), Krauthammer (1990/1991), and Freedman (1991/1992).

[2] In his 1953 inaugural address, Dwight D. Eisenhower exclaimed, "Freedom is pitted against slavery; lightness against dark. . . . Conceiving the defense of freedom, like freedom itself, to be one and indivisible, we hold all continents and peoples in equal regard and honor."

of freedom. This is the position not only of the current administration but also that of its predecessors and, we would argue, almost certainly its successors.

But settling the big question—What should be the central political motivation for U.S. foreign policy?—leaves unanswered many subsidiary but important questions regarding how, where, and in what manner the policy will be implemented. For example, is the United States committed to supporting all democratic movements in the world, even in places like China? Should the United States support the development of democratic opposition movements in countries where none now exist? Should the United States seek the overthrow, perhaps by force of arms, of all despotic regimes?

As a result, when George W. Bush declared on January 20, 2005, that "it is the policy of the United States to seek and support the growth of democratic movements and institutions in every nation and culture, with the ultimate goal of ending tyranny in our world," he reignited a debate not so much about the broader goal of promoting freedom and democracy but more about the specific applications and, in particular, the experiment under way in Iraq.

Of course, the idea of promoting freedom and democracy is not new, either for this president or for the United States.[3] Indeed, the roots of this strategy are drawn from long experience and from America's great 20th-century struggles against fascism and communism.[4] But the roots also are found in the policies of Bush's immediate predecessors: William Clinton and George H. W. Bush. Both presidents saw it as America's mission to bring freedom to others in the world, and both

---

[3] The debate over the importance of supporting democracy abroad is nearly as old as the republic itself. U.S. foreign policy during George Washington's second term as president was dominated by a debate over whether the United States should lend support to revolutionary France or remain neutral. Thomas Jefferson favored U.S. intervention to support the fledgling democracy, while Alexander Hamilton argued, successfully, for neutrality. (See White House, undated.)

[4] Recall, for example, Franklin Roosevelt's "Four Freedoms" (Roosevelt, 1941). Consider also John F. Kennedy's inaugural address (1961): "Let every nation know, whether it wishes us well or ill, that we shall pay any price, bear any burden, meet any hardship, support any friend, oppose any foe to assure the survival and the success of liberty."

acted to reinforce the gains of freedom where they could. For George H. W. Bush, a key goal was to "strengthen and enlarge the commonwealth of free nations that share a commitment to democracy and individual rights."[5] In practical terms, this meant helping facilitate a democratic transition in the Philippines, providing tangible support to the new democracies of Eastern Europe after the collapse of the Warsaw Pact and the fall of the Soviet Union, and providing support to democratic forces within Russia itself. For William Clinton, who established as one of three national security goals "to promote democracy abroad,"[6] it meant securing the gains of freedom by enlarging NATO, fostering new relationships in the Americas, supporting the democratic movement in South Africa, developing relations in the Caucasus and Central Asia, and supporting democratic elections throughout East Asia.[7]

America's New Grand Strategy?

Extending the reach of freedom formed the centerpiece of the West's response to the immediate end of the Cold War—supporting "a Europe whole and free" encompassing the former members of the Warsaw Pact and Soviet Union and including the unification of Germany. It was the basis for U.S. policy in Central and Eastern Europe and in Central and South America throughout the 1990s. It motivated the U.S. response to support the end of apartheid in South Africa. It guided U.S. interactions throughout large portions of Asia, China being an important exception. It has been a source of friction in the greater Middle East. And it has remained an important aspiration for U.S. policy in the Caucasus, Central Asia, and large portions of Africa.

---

[5] See White House (1991). For a discussion of the elder Bush's views at the time, see Bush and Scowcroft (1998).

[6] Clinton's other goals were "to credibly sustain our security with military forces that are ready to fight" and "to bolster America's economic revitalization." (See White House, 1994.)

[7] For a separate discussion, see Albright (2003).

Now, most importantly, the assumption that democracy is the foundation of lasting peace motivates a central component of the nation's response to the attacks of September 11, 2001. Not only did the United States respond to the tragic events by bringing its might against those who perpetrated the attacks, it also displaced the Taliban regime that hosted al Qaeda and sought—and still seeks today—to leave in its place a free Afghan people governed by democratic principles. Within little more than a year of bringing down the Taliban regime, the United States set for itself similar goals in Iraq: to free the Iraqi people from a despotic regime that had repeatedly threatened its neighbors, attacked its own citizens, and was purported to possess weapons of mass destruction.

And it is here that the strategy of the Bush administration has taken an important and arguably fundamentally different turn from that of its predecessors. In response to the terrorist attacks of September 11, 2001, this administration was no longer content simply to await opportunities to extend freedom as such opportunities arose; it would now commit itself to creating opportunities for exporting freedom, even if, at times, that should require the force of arms. If America's freedoms were to be protected at home, so argued the administration, freedom needed to establish broader and deeper roots abroad. The defeat of Saddam Hussein was seen as the first step toward reshaping the broader Middle East to introduce more liberal institutions and thereby ameliorate the conditions that spawned terrorism.[8] At least for this administration, the link between freedom abroad, especially in troubled regions, and U.S. security crystallized into the basis for long-term strategic action.[9]

Whether the experiment in Iraq succeeds or not will have a large bearing on whether the United States will engage again in trying to

---

[8]   As this text was being written, American leaders were calling for free elections in Egypt and arguing aggressively for democratic reforms throughout the greater Middle East. For a discussion on the near-term prospects for liberalization in Egypt, see Diehl (2005). For a brief discussion of pressures within Saudi Arabia, see "Should the West Always Be Worried if Islamists Win Elections?" (2005).

[9]   For a separate, impassioned discussion on the case for spreading democracy and freedom abroad, see Sharansky (2004).

establish representative forms of government, through force of arms, in places where they did not before exist. But success or failure in Iraq probably should be separated from the broader goal of promoting freedom and democracy, which is well grounded in America's historical experience, which has motivated the foreign policy of all three post–Cold War presidents and which, in light of America's current security situation, will likely remain a key goal for any future administration. Said differently, even if America is not likely to engage again anytime soon in an operation to forcibly remove a hostile regime and replace it with a representative government, as in Iraq, it will still seek to promote freedom and democracy as a key foreign policy goal and as an important response to the threat of global terrorism.

Indeed, to the extent that the United States has adopted a new grand strategy as the successor to containment, promoting freedom and democracy would be that strategy. And although U.S. leaders will differ over the means with which to implement the strategy, it seems likely that future American presidents will continue to pursue it, much as did their predecessors.[10] The when, where, and how of promoting democracy are likely to be debated much more than the issue of why.

The strategy for promoting democracy and freedom can and will take many forms:

- providing support to nonviolent democratic movements throughout the globe, such as the Velvet, Rose, Orange, and Cedar revolutions[11]
- providing aid and encouragement to democratic regimes in newly independent countries

---

[10] As an illustration, in the 2004 U.S. presidential campaign, John Kerry (2004) argued,

> we will promote the development of free and democratic societies throughout the Arab and Muslim World. Millions of people there share our values of human rights, and our hopes for a better life for the next generation. . . . We must reach out to them and yes we must promote democracy. I will be clear with repressive governments in the region that we expect to see them change—not just for our sake but for their own survival.

[11] This, of course, refers to the democratic movements in the Czech Republic, Georgia, Ukraine, and Lebanon, respectively.

- when appropriate, extending security commitments to emerging democracies
- pressuring, by limiting aid and support, friendly regimes that restrict freedom
- aiming to defeat the groups, movements, and individuals that threaten the freedom and security of others, particularly global terrorist organizations
- enforcing "responsible sovereignty" by challenging regimes to extend freedoms within their own boundaries and to prohibit outlaw activity, especially terrorism
- *in extremis* and when feasible, ending the rule of regimes that most flagrantly violate the rights of their citizens and that deliberately harbor terrorist groups.

Much of the work needed to support this strategy will be done by diplomats, philosophers, educators, political advisors, economic advisors, technical advisors, communicators, and specialists from a wide array of fields. These various fields and areas of expertise merit the same or even greater attention than the military capabilities that are detailed elsewhere in this monograph. If the role of the military is to create the space for democracy to succeed, it is the role of these disciplines to create the conditions for success.

There is no question that this strategy comes with controversy and risk; the Iraqi insurgency, for example, is an unintended consequence of the U.S.-led effort to depose Saddam Hussein. Americans themselves, although unquestionably supportive of their freedoms at home, can be divided over the extent to which the United States should not only be a beacon for freedom abroad but also play the role of liberator and enforcer.[12] Likewise, some long-time U.S. friends and allies are concerned about the spillover effects of pushing too hard, too fast to open societies that have long been under repressive rule. Indeed, leaders

---

[12] For example, Chicago Council on Foreign Relations (2004) reported that only 14 percent of those surveyed thought that "helping to bring a democratic form of government to other nations" was a very important foreign policy goal; 27 percent of the people thought this goal was not important. This compares with 73 percent of those surveyed who thought "preventing the spread of nuclear weapons" was a very important foreign policy goal.

of some pro-American states are concerned not only about the effects abroad but also about the effects instability and upheaval abroad could have within their own societies.[13] Some of America's new partners are grateful for its support for their own causes but are reluctant to assume the risks of supporting U.S. goals for freedom in other lands.[14] And, of course, several of America's long-time partners—Egypt and Saudi Arabia come to mind—and new partners in the war on terrorism—Pakistan and Uzbekistan, to name two—are at best ambivalent toward America's goals for freedom and at worst strongly against them, as the collapse of relations with Uzbekistan demonstrates.[15]

New Friends, New Commitments, New Tensions

This new U.S. strategy has won many important supporters and friends. Key allies, such as Great Britain, Japan, and Australia, firmly back America's goals, even as debate about such support continues within their own societies. New allies and partners, such as Poland, Romania, and Georgia, have pledged support to these goals and have provided visible assistance, in the form of troops, to aid in advancing them.

But just as new partners are prepared to provide support, they will also rely on America's commitment and support for their own security. Political and economic liberalization in Central and Eastern Europe was followed by security commitments in the form of North Atlantic Treaty Organization (NATO) enlargement. For now, these commitments come at a relatively low cost to the United States, given the relatively benign circumstances in Europe. But the future remains uncertain, and new challenges could place additional demands on America and its NATO partners, thus raising the stakes on what it actually means to enlarge the alliance.

---

[13] See, for example, Rabasa et al. (2004); see also Zakaria (2003).

[14] For example, consider declines in support for providing troops in Iraq. See, for example, Wright and White (2005).

[15] See "Egypt Criticizes U.S. 'Democracy' Initiative, Jordan, Qatar, Israel Welcome" (2004). See also "Should the West Always Be Worried if Islamists Win Elections?" (2005).

The same is true in Asia. Although America's democratic partners in Asia generally are more prosperous and thus able to provide more effectively for their own security, security challenges in Asia also are more difficult, as will be discussed later. Just as many of America's Asian allies are prepared to support its goals for freedom beyond Asia, the United States should also expect that these allies will look for stronger U.S. commitments to deal with mounting security challenges within the region where they live.

The United States is today deeply involved in Afghanistan and Iraq. Long-term security relationships have not yet been the subject of open discussion, but we should expect that, as political institutions mature in these countries, political leaders in both countries might desire to engage the United States in a dialogue about how to protect new-found freedoms and provide for long-term security, recognizing that the desired support may take the form of financial and material assistance rather than the physical presence of U.S. forces. Alternatively, these countries might seek to separate themselves from American influences, which in turn could produce new security concerns.

Even when America's allies and partners are prepared to provide support for its broader goals of freedom, such support will inevitably be conditional. In some cases, the risks that the United States is asking others to share are not always ones that its partners are prepared to accept. And when they do accept a role in sharing these risks, these partners, particularly the newest ones, generally seek something tangible in return, such as money, which is relatively easy to provide; special status, which can be more difficult and may not always be that meaningful (note the proliferation of formal non-NATO ally status); or a commitment to deal with their own security problems, which can be the most difficult, particularly when it may involve the United States taking sides among potential partners.

Sharing risks also means sharing in the rewards. Allies and partners that share in America's risks want a much greater voice in the decisions being made. They will have a stake in the outcomes the United States seeks—indeed, they may want very different outcomes and therefore will want to shape events in conference rooms as well as on battlefields. U.S. leaders, in turn, will need to respect these desires and create modalities so that those who share in the risks have a voice in shaping the outcomes.

Others, of course, are deeply conflicted about America's new strategy. Some U.S. partners, particularly its partners in the war on terrorism, worry that the U.S. pursuit of freedom will bring about the fall of its purported friends. Following his ousting in the Rose Revolution in Georgia, Eduard Shevardnadze is said to have warned his fellow leaders in the Caucasus and Central Asia that U.S. support for internal reforms ultimately could lead to their own demise. Although these leaders are prepared to partner with the United States to achieve very specific aims, they may be wary of its ultimate goals; witness Islam Karimov's change of heart in Uzbekistan. Observers throughout the Middle East certainly harbor similar apprehensions.

These apprehensions are not limited to small, regional states. China has expressed strong resentment of U.S. calls for freedom. While generally supportive of the American desire to defeat global terrorism, China's leadership remains suspicious of broader U.S. ambitions for freedom and its demands that human rights be respected,[16] especially if that were to mean the end of communist party rule. And China has expressed grave concerns over calls for freedom in Taiwan, especially when the calls are linked to support for Taiwan's independence.

Russia, too, is suspicious of Washington's motives, both for Russia itself and for the area that Russia considers its "near abroad."[17] Russian leaders remain concerned that, as Washington establishes closer relationships with states in the Caucasus and Central Asia, it will encroach on areas of traditional Russian influence and foment instability that could directly affect Russia itself. Although Vladimir Putin recently stated that there is no turning back on Russian democracy,[18] Russia objects to Washington asserting its views about how freedoms should be manifested within Russian society.

---

[16] Information Office of the State Council of the People's Republic of China (2005).

[17] Russia considers the "near abroad" to be the other 14 former Soviet republics that had declared their independence by the time the Soviet Union broke up at the end of 1991.

[18] Putin (2005).

More recently, China and Russia have sought to cooperate in setting limits to the reach of U.S. efforts to promote democracy abroad.[19]

What Does This Mean for America's Armed Forces?

America's armed forces have been and will continue to be affected deeply by America's new strategy. As the United States assumes new commitments, its military forces will be called on to support and defend these commitments.[20] As the United States supports freedom and independence for others and works to discredit and defeat global militants, its forces will be called on to advise, support, train, and assist the forces of like-minded states—what we call "direct" and "indirect" stability operations. As the United States and its partners seek to halt the proliferation of dangerous weapons and technologies to hostile regimes—which, in many instances, are the regimes most hostile to its goals for freedom—its forces will be called on to provide intelligence; track the movement of people and goods; intercept banned weapons and cargo; and, occasionally, strike with force against weapons, facilities, and command-and-control complexes. And finally, in rare but not unimaginable circumstances, U.S. forces could again be called on to be liberators and enforcers of freedom abroad.

Add these tasks to more traditional roles of protecting America at home, defending Americans abroad, protecting the commons (maritime, air, space, and cyberspace), securing U.S. allies (now against a much wider array of challenges), and projecting U.S. power to defend against aggression and coercion, and it becomes clear that the nation's armed forces will be called on to conduct an ever more diverse set of missions and activities. How to provide the forces and capabilities most

---

[19] For more on Russian and Chinese cooperation, see Holley (2005).

[20] As one simple example, when NATO grew first from 16 to 19 nations, then from 19 to 26 nations, there came with that growth a new U.S. military commitment to work with NATO's new partners. And while this will not likely require significant new presence of U.S. military forces, it will place significant demands on U.S. forces to interact, train, and exercise with all 26 NATO member nations.

needed to meet the demands of these requirements is the focus of the chapters that follow.

CHAPTER TWO

Conflict in the Post Post–Cold War World

While U.S. grand strategy is one important source of change in the geopolitical environment, it is not the sole, or even the primary, force at work; the world has dynamics and logics of its own that strategy must accommodate or change. While the security environment may exhibit a rough equilibrium for protracted periods, it is subject to occasional and often unpredictable eruptions of change. The world experienced one such seismic shock in the early 1990s when the Soviet Union imploded and the Cold War, which had dominated U.S. security thinking and military planning for four decades, came unexpectedly to an end. Even 15 years later, the American security establishment has yet to adapt fully to the aftershocks of this sudden, seismic shift in the geopolitical landscape. Nevertheless, however complete or incomplete the Pentagon's transition from its Cold War mind-set, it today confronts another set of new circumstances that will require major adjustments in institutions, forces, and posture. The ambitious strategy outlined in the preceding chapter is motivated in large measure by these challenges.

The symbolic mileposts for this latest transition are, of course, the September 11, 2001, terrorist attacks on New York City and Washington, D.C., but the changes were in train long before that day. The threat of which the strikes on the World Trade Center and the Pentagon are emblematic is just one of three challenges the nation must confront: terrorism and insurgency, nuclear proliferation, and the emergence of China. All stem to some extent from the diffusion of technological know-how and power, including the power of lethal and large-scale violence, associated with the processes of globalization now under way.

Terrorism and Insurgency

In the forefront of the nation's security concerns today are, of course, the related problems of terrorism and insurgency, which feed on underlying problems of unmet expectations, weak or illegitimate governments, and conflicts of identity. Al Qaeda's attacks on the United States and its allies—not just on September 11, 2001, but also in Spain, Turkey, the United Kingdom, East Africa, Saudi Arabia, Indonesia, and elsewhere—demonstrate that small but motivated groups of individuals can inflict severe damage at places and times that generally cannot be anticipated. The experience in Iraq, meanwhile, has reminded Americans of the costs and difficulties of fighting against an insurgent opponent that is well integrated into the local environment and capable of disrupting and distorting normal social, economic, and political life. Today, the United States is engaged in what may prove to be a prolonged and wide-ranging struggle against what some observers have called a "global insurgency"—a nexus of terrorists, guerrillas, criminals, and others who reject the global order promoted by the West and seek to undermine American power and influence. These enemies pose serious challenges: They lack well-defined and easily identifiable centers of gravity; they are resilient and adaptive; they are deeply unpredictable; and they are ambitious in their strategic goals.

The challenges inherent in this confrontation are manifold. To begin with, the threat is global in two respects. First, it is apparent that sophisticated terrorist groups, such as al Qaeda, have developed "networking" capabilities that allow widely dispersed individuals and cells to work together in mounting complex attacks. Planning and preparations for the September 11 hijackings, for example, appear to have involved operatives in North America, Europe, Africa, the Middle East, Central Asia, and South Asia.[1] Second, it is almost impossible to rule out a priori any potential target from being at risk. We know little about the targeting processes or preferences of our adversaries save what we have learned from the proverbial "flaming data," which suggest that terrorists and insurgents will strike at such diverse things as

---

[1] See Rabasa et al. (2006).

power lines, discothèques, and the military headquarters of the most powerful nation on earth.[2] Any strategy for countering terrorism that pays insufficient heed to these qualities of the opposition runs the risk of pursuing little more than a lethal, expensive, and most likely futile effort to defeat a proactive adversary with a completely reactive strategy.

Second, because the threat is adaptable and can manifest itself almost anywhere, point defense becomes a "mug's game." There are some highly exposed targets—U.S. embassies in troubled areas, for example—and others of sufficient importance (facilities associated with critical consequence-management functions come to mind) to merit some degree of protection. But in general, attempts to protect everything will likely result in protecting nothing, and the best that can be done is to try to close the most obvious avenues of attack (pre-September 11 airline security being the most notorious example) while taking the fight to the enemy.

Finally, the struggle will be a long one and will assume many forms and shapes. We have already seen—in Afghanistan, Iraq, Central Asia, the Philippines, and elsewhere—how individual missions can last years and can involve anywhere from dozens to tens of thousands of personnel in roles ranging from support and training to sustained direct combat. U.S. military forces will be called on to mount and sustain multiple prolonged operations of very different sizes and purposes in widely separated parts of the world. In a sense, we may be seeing a redefinition of what *forward presence* means: In addition to the familiar mechanized brigades and fighter wings deployed at well-developed bases in allied countries, U.S. forces now will be scattered around the world, usually in smaller deployments, working to train and advise their host-country counterparts. This is a very different kind of tasking, and carrying it out successfully will call for new kinds of capabilities from each of the services.

---

2   There has, of course, been no lack of studies on the future of terrorism since September 2001. A brief but quite trenchant one is Hoffman (2003). See also Cragin and Daly (2004).

The New Nuclear Equation

New challenges are arising, too, in the realm of interstate warfare—what the Pentagon has sometimes referred to as *major combat operations*. For the past century, these "big wars" have generally been the focal point of U.S. defense planning, whether the opponent was projected to be Japan or Germany in the 1930s, the Soviet Union and its Warsaw Pact satellites throughout the Cold War, or Iraq and North Korea since 1990. When called on to fight these enemies, U.S. forces have proven to be very successful, especially over the past 15 years. Future major combat operations will be quite different, however, from the 1991 and 2003 wars with Iraq. One major component of that difference is the role nuclear weapons are likely to play in future crises.

For decades, the global nonproliferation regime has been the backbone of efforts to halt or slow the spread of nuclear weapons. A key aspect of this regime's success was that, for most of the nuclear age, both the weapons and the know-how for manufacturing them remained in the hands of nations that, by and large, had little if any incentive to spread either around.[3] The Nuclear Non-Proliferation Treaty formalized this situation, committing the then-nuclear powers to cooperate in limiting the diffusion of nuclear weapons. As was perhaps inevitable, however, recent years have seen the acquisition of nuclear arms by countries that have proven less-responsible managers of their new knowledge and capabilities. While there is as yet no available evidence to suggest that complete and functioning nuclear weapons have changed hands, or even that substantial quantities of weapon-grade fissile materials have been transferred, weapon technology has certainly leaked, either as a deliberate act of state policy, as is likely the case with North Korea, or as a result of individual actions, as demonstrated by the behavior of the A. Q. Khan "network" in Pakistan. Either way, the nuclear genie is today well out of the bottle, and prudent U.S. planners at both the strategic and operational levels must seriously contemplate the implica-

---

[3] The Soviets, for example, were so concerned about the possible spread of nuclear technology that they reneged on a deal to provide a prototype weapon to China, a decision that cemented the split between Moscow and Beijing that wound up outlasting the Soviet Union itself. (See Nathan and Ross, 1998.)

tions of a proliferated world for U.S. concepts of national defense and power projection.

The success that the nuclear-armed parties to the Cold War had in avoiding nuclear use was due to more than the horrific consequences of a war involving nuclear weapons. Two other important factors pertained: One was that the sides' mutual interest in avoiding a potentially cataclysmic confrontation far outweighed their stakes in any of the disagreements that would inevitably arise between them; the other was that neither side would deliberately provoke a deep crisis between them. Within these broad constraints, both Moscow and Washington sometimes determined the boundaries of acceptable behavior by pushing them, most dramatically in 1962 when Khrushchev almost catastrophically underestimated the United States' reaction to the placement of Soviet missiles in Cuba. But, for the most part, the Cold War adversaries respected the rules of the deterrence game. Indeed, the United States imposed fairly substantial constraints on its military operations in both Korea and Vietnam out of a perceived need to avoid provoking escalatory responses from Moscow or Beijing.

Neither of these two foundations of a relatively robust deterrent relationship may hold between the United States and a nuclear-armed North Korea or other similar foes.[4] In the case of Korea, for example, the risk of conflict may not be determined solely, or even primarily, by Pyongyang's external circumstances. Internationally isolated, desperately poor, and politically underdeveloped to the point of self-caricature, it is not implausible that North Korea may prove to be so unstable that, confronting some domestic crisis, it could strike out against outside enemies, real or perceived. Even the most conciliatory U.S. policy might prove inadequate to prevent such an outcome with its accompanying risk of nuclear use.

Yet, U.S. policy toward North Korea seems unlikely to be conciliatory. Unlike the situation in the Cold War, the United States may have interests outside the immediate confines of a cross–demilitarized

---

[4] This discussion will focus on the problems posed by a North Korean bomb. We believe, and argue elsewhere, that a similar logic would inform the U.S. position vis-à-vis a hostile and nuclear-armed Iran or another regional adversary with nuclear arms.

zone confrontation that outweigh the risks of a confrontation with Pyongyang. For example, concerns over proliferation of nuclear materials, technology, or know-how could prompt Washington to seek a showdown with the North, especially if there is a risk of a terrorist group, such as al Qaeda, being the recipient of North Korean nuclear largesse. Under such circumstances, Kim Jong Il would almost certainly, and probably correctly, believe that his rule and his life were at risk and thus could be motivated to use every tool at his disposal, including nuclear weapons, in his attempts to ward off American pressure. Thus, the constraints on escalation that the nuclear powers have long relied on in dealing with one another may not apply in North Korea, where the stakes of any profound confrontation with the United States are apt to be perceived by the leadership in Pyongyang as mortal. Whether the crisis erupts because of internal convulsions within North Korea or because external pressures have been applied to it, U.S. planners must contend with the very real possibility that any future war on the Korean peninsula could include the use of nuclear weapons. This raises serious political and operational problems.

The most nettlesome political challenges a nuclear North Korea poses stem from the reversal of the classic extended deterrence logic that long prevailed between the United States and its allies. Throughout the Cold War, the United States linked its nuclear weapons to the security of its core allies by threatening retaliation against the Soviet Union for any attack on, for example, West Germany or Japan. In doing so, the United States was attempting to protect important and shared interests—the security of its partners—by exposing itself to a risk of Soviet counterattack against which its allies offered no defense. Today in Northeast Asia, the situation may be reversed. In pursuit of common goals, such as nonproliferation, the United States may be asking Japan and South Korea—who would be directly endangered by any North Korean nuclear arsenal—to assume risks against which Washington can offer no viable defense or credible response.[5] The

---

[5]   The United States has obvious quantitative and qualitative nuclear superiority over North Korea and could threaten massive retaliation against it in response to attacks on U.S. allies in Asia. However, given that the North Korean leadership would probably believe that their

complexities that this turnaround of risk dynamics could introduce into alliance relations, and the attendant basing and access difficulties that it could cause, should be of concern to U.S. strategists and planners. The coercive effects of nuclear weapons in the hands of adversaries could be substantial: Whether or not North Korea, for example, explicitly brandished its arsenal as a Northeast Asian crisis unfolded, both Seoul and Tokyo would have to factor the extraordinary risks associated with confronting a nuclear power into their behavior, with potentially harmful consequences for U.S. political and military freedom of action.

Operationally, of course, nuclear weapons will give North Korea offensive options against both military and civilian targets within range of its delivery systems, which likely will include most of Japan in addition to all of South Korea. Key U.S. bases at Camp Humphreys, Osan, and Kunsan in South Korea and in Misawa, Kadena, Atsugi, and Iwakuni, among others, in Japan will be at risk, as will such population centers as Seoul, Pusan, and Tokyo.[6] While active defenses and hardening could enhance the survivability of military installations and, to a lesser extent, cities, there is, for the foreseeable future, no means of assuring that either type of target could be protected against nuclear attack.

The Rise of China

The reemergence of China as a true "great power" is a third major force that will shape the security environment in coming years. The world's

---

survival was at stake no matter what course they were to choose, it is not clear that merely changing the means of their threatened destruction would have a profound deterrent effect. Further, in a fight that is not for the survival of the United States, nuclear attacks that carry with them the prospect of immense casualties among the adversary's civilian population could seem morally reprehensible to U.S. leaders and citizens alike. Finally, creating further devastation than would exist absent nuclear strikes (indeed, even absent any war at all) would have profound and negative consequences in the postwar period.

[6] For a recent revelation on North Korea's nuclear capabilities, see Graham and Kessler (2005).

most populous country, China has over the past three decades built the planet's second-largest national economy.[7] Beijing's reputation has also grown as the country has transitioned from the Maoist period to being a dynamic and modern actor on the world stage.

From a security perspective, the growing power of China's military is a fundamental challenge to the existing order in East Asia. Since the end of the Cold War, the United States has stood unrivalled as the preeminent military power in East Asia and has likewise been the ultimate guarantor of stability in the region. Even if Beijing's integration into the global community continues to be a peaceful process by and large, the emergence of a large and modern Chinese military is altering the Asian balance of power in unsettling ways. Helping shape modern China's debut on the world stage into a positive development while simultaneously hedging against the possibility that it could turn more hostile is a major and enduring challenge for U.S. security policy.

The status of Taiwan is the principal issue of contention in the Sino-U.S. relationship. While the United States withdrew from its defense treaty with Taipei in 1979, the Taiwan Relations Act has required every administration since to pay close attention to the military balance across the Taiwan Strait. U.S. arms sales to Taiwan—which the Chinese regime considers a renegade province—have engendered periodic and almost predictable eruptions of outrage from Beijing, but to little avail. Through it all, U.S. policy on the China-Taiwan issue has remained remarkably consistent, calling on both sides to keep the peace and to resolve the question of sovereignty over the island in a manner consistent with the will of the people of Taiwan. Today, the status of Taiwan is the most neuralgic point in the Sino-U.S. relationship and one of the most dangerous flashpoints in the world.[8]

---

[7] According to the 2004 edition of the Central Intelligence Agency's *World Factbook*, China's 2003 gross domestic product of about $6.5 trillion trailed only that of the United States and was nearly double that of third-place Japan.

[8] As China's strength and self-confidence grow, it is possible that other points of contention will arise between Beijing and Washington. To take a current example, China has conflicting objectives in dealing with North Korea. On one hand, China desires a nonnuclear Korean peninsula; on the other, concerns over the likely consequences of any unrest in North Korea lead China to strongly prefer a stable regime in Pyongyang. For the United States, the goal of

The cross-strait dilemma has been heightened in recent years by the complex and deep changes China is undergoing. Increased prosperity has turned out to be a double-edged sword for China's communist leaders, however. On the one hand, China's new wealth means greater regional and global influence and creates resources for building all the elements of the "comprehensive national power" Beijing seeks. On the other, the overtly capitalist aspects of the new economy have once and for all vanquished the gods of Chinese Marxism-Leninism without offering satisfactory replacements. Beijing's solution has been to seek regime legitimacy by delivering continued economic growth and through appeals to nationalism.

So far, their strategy has succeeded. China's economy continues to turn in impressive growth year after year. And, although it faces some real challenges managing, for example, the sharply skewed distribution of wealth between the modernized coastal provinces and the less-developed interior regions, a return to pre-reform ways of doing business seems unthinkable. Similarly, the leadership has scored two historic successes by achieving the return of Hong Kong and Macao, both lost to European powers in the precommunist era. The last colonial "humiliation" to be rectified by China is the loss of Taiwan, which was ceded to Japan in the 1895 Treaty of Shimonoseki that ended the first Sino-Japanese War.

Since at least the mid-1990s, Beijing has had concerns that Taiwan may be slipping out of its grasp. While only a minority on the island advocate outright independence—a step that China has repeatedly warned could result in an all-out attack on Taiwan—the Chinese leadership fears that Taiwan's increasing democratization and the growing "Taiwanization" of its culture and politics are pulling it further and further from the mainland. While China is unlikely to risk war to

---

denying North Korea a nuclear capability trumps any concerns over internal stability there. While it is unlikely that such differences would cause the United States and China to come to blows, the example does point to the possibility that multiple sources of friction could emerge as China becomes more vocal about and active in the defense of its perceived interests in Asia and elsewhere. As is the case with North Korean nuclear weapons, these issues will complicate not just Sino-U.S. relations but also U.S. ties with such allies and friends as Japan and South Korea.

compel unification per se, most analysts agree that Beijing is serious when it says that it will consider using force to prevent a final break between Beijing and Taipei. To this end, the People's Liberation Army (PLA) has been tasked with developing a range of military options for pressuring and, if necessary, conquering Taiwan.[9]

While no longer bound by treaty to Taiwan's defense, the United States remains the third main player in the cross-strait security dynamic. Isolated from other major providers of military hardware, Taiwan depends heavily on the United States to help it maintain a defensive posture against the mainland. Moreover, the Chinese leadership probably regards direct U.S. intervention in a China-Taiwan conflict as highly likely. Accordingly, China's military modernization, which has been under way for many years but has accelerated in the past five years, has two primary goals: deterring or preventing an effective U.S. military intervention in a cross-strait military offensive and compelling an isolated Taiwanese leadership to surrender. To achieve this, the PLA has undertaken to update both its strategy and its equipment.

Today, China no longer regards the threat of either a nuclear attack or a massive land invasion as its primary security concerns. Rather, a new approach has crystallized that emphasizes limited offensive power projection in areas on China's periphery, such as the Taiwan Strait. This doctrine, sometimes referred to as "limited war under high-tech conditions," emphasizes both the subordination of military to political goals and the need to achieve a military decision quickly, before international pressure can force an end to hostilities. Such a doctrine has obvious appeal in terms of helping the PLA deal with the threat of U.S. intervention: The Chinese would hope to exploit the time it would take the United States to decide on a course of action and then mobilize and deploy its forces. Ideally, from Beijing's point of view, Taiwan would be subdued before anything more than token U.S. military power could be brought to bear, leaving Washington to decide whether the costs

---

[9] There is a broad and diverse literature on the subject of China's military modernization (see, for example, Shambaugh, 2004, and Crane et al., 2005). A less rigorous but perhaps more entertaining perspective can be found in Bernstein and Munro (1998).

of reversing a new status quo would be justified by the U.S. interests engaged.

To deal with any U.S. forces that do attempt to come to Taiwan's defense, China has focused considerable attention on developing and fielding what are often referred to in American defense circles as "anti-access" capabilities. These capabilities run a wide gamut, from offensive information operations and counterspace, to advanced fighters and air defenses, to long-range strike systems able to target air bases, ports, and naval forces. The PLA's goal would not be to defeat the U.S. military in a traditional, set-piece confrontation but rather to keep it at arm's length just long enough—perhaps a few days, certainly not more than a week or two—to bring Taiwan to heel.[10]

For U.S. planners, a China-Taiwan scenario presents multiple difficulties. The western Pacific is vast, and there is little territory to which land-based forces, including air forces, can stake a claim. And the installations that do exist will be increasingly threatened by Chinese offensive capabilities. Today, the PLA has deployed over 600 ballistic missiles opposite Taiwan, a number of which could be fired at the key U.S. Air Force base in the region, Kadena Air Base on Okinawa.[11] The PLA Navy, meanwhile, is operating increasingly sophisticated and well-armed surface and submarine forces. While they are no match for those of the U.S. Navy in a full-scale fleet action, early arriving

---

[10] Even with recent, substantial increases in military spending, China's defense buildup appears to be unfolding at a deliberate pace; the best available estimate for China's total military spending—both official and unofficial—in 2003 is $31 billion to 38 billion. Given reasonable assumptions about both the pace of China's continued economic growth (which could slow) and its ability to mobilize resources for defense, the number can be expected to grow to over $180 billion (fiscal year [FY] 2001 dollars) by 2025 and could exceed $400 billion. China's cumulative investment in research and development and procurement from 2003 through 2025 will likely fall in the range of roughly $600 billion to 1.2 trillion, or one-fourth to one-half the total the United States invested in similar accounts between 1981 and 2003. These levels of expenditure mean that the PLA can expect to enjoy substantial capability improvements in coming years. For a thorough analysis of China's current and future defense spending, see Crane et al. (2005, pp. 133–134).

[11] The number of short- and medium-range missiles in Beijing's arsenal is also growing, as is their accuracy and the sophistication and variety of conventional warheads deployed on them.

U.S. Navy forces—perhaps a single carrier strike group—would confront a multifaceted threat that could either keep them away from the immediate area of operations or compel them to dedicate a substantial portion of their combat power to self-defense instead of the defense of Taiwan. Either way, the Chinese would have accomplished what they set out to do.

Coping with growing Chinese power, like dealing with nuclear weapons, will be far from easy. Helping defend civilian and military targets on Taiwan (and in Japan) from barrages of modern, accurate Chinese ballistic and cruise missiles will require offensive and defensive capabilities that do not presently exist. The PLA presents threats to U.S. air, space, and naval operations the likes of which have not been encountered since the fall of the Soviet Union. And, in a conflict with Taiwan, if the Chinese are able to enforce the kind of compressed timeline toward which their doctrine suggests that they will strive, the United States may have only hours or days to mount an effective response. Any Chinese attack on Taiwan remains a high-risk gamble on Beijing's part; however, as the PLA's capabilities grow, the risks to the United States and Taiwan increase in parallel.[12]

Welcome to the Post Post–Cold War World

In this chapter, we have explored the diverse kinds of challenges that the United States will likely encounter in the new era that we have dubbed "the post post–Cold War world." They can be summarized as follows:

---

[12] As China's projected timelines for subduing Taiwan grow shorter, the time-distance problems the United States would face—its closest base to Taiwan is Kadena, 450 nmi away and threatened by Chinese surface-to-surface missiles—will grow. Honolulu is over 4,200 nmi from Taiwan; steaming at 25 kts, an aircraft carrier deploying from Pearl Harbor would take about a week to reach Taiwan. Land-based aircraft can deploy more rapidly, of course, but, as noted, there are few bases for them in the region. With adequate air-to-air refueling support, fighters can operate out of Guam, but from that distance—about 1,300 nmi—the round-trip transit time for a sortie is on the order of six hours. Missions of such long duration reduce the sortie rates that can be achieved by a fleet of a given size and could impede U.S. Air Force operations in defense of Taiwan.

- subnational or transnational groups—insurgencies and terrorist organizations—able to launch highly destructive attacks against U.S. interests and citizens and those of its allies
- state adversaries armed with nuclear weapons and an inclination to employ them or believably threaten to do so
- state adversaries—China being the prime example—equipped with "antiaccess" capabilities and strategies intended to hold U.S. power at bay.

Coping with any one of these problems is demanding; dealing with all three simultaneously will likely require a substantial rethinking of how U.S. military forces are organized, trained, and equipped, to say nothing of the roles that the United States and its allies need to adopt to provide for their security. In the next chapter, we present ideas about what forces built to succeed in this complex and dangerous world might look like.

CHAPTER THREE

Toward a New Division of Labor

The grand strategy that the United States has adopted and the difficult challenges the nation will confront in the coming years beget a wide range of missions for its armed forces. They also call for different types of arrangements within U.S. alliances and partnerships, with more focus needed on new and emerging missions and a different focus on more-familiar missions in light of emerging threats.

For the purposes of sizing and shaping the nation's general-purpose and special operations forces (SOF), the following five missions are most relevant:

- countering terrorist and insurgent groups abroad
- helping to bring stability to emerging democracies
- deterring and defeating regional adversaries
- dissuading military competition in Asia, specifically by countering Chinese military power
- helping to protect the U.S. homeland.

This chapter examines each of these missions in turn, identifying the types of capabilities that will likely be called for to accomplish each one.[1] It then offers some insights about the overall levels of mili-

---

[1] Although the analysis in this chapter follows from our recommendations on strategy, many of the specific actions we recommend here and in later chapters could also be made on the basis of efficiency.

tary capability that are appropriate for meeting the demands of U.S. strategy.[2]

Countering Terrorists and Insurgent Groups Abroad

Although the armed forces of the United States do not bear sole responsibility for protecting the nation against terrorist attacks, they do play important roles, and these roles have placed new demands on the armed forces. Nowhere are these roles more evident than when a foreign government shares the U.S. interest in eradicating terrorism but lacks the capabilities to do so effectively on its own.[3] Such states span a wide gamut, from traditional security partners, such as the Philippines, to states with which the United States lacks a long history of security cooperation, such as Yemen. Some, like the governments of Uzbekistan and the Philippines, seek to prosecute aggressive operations against terrorist groups on their territories. Others, such as Sudan and Somalia, may be more ambivalent or may simply be incapable of mounting effective operations. Given this wide range of potential operating environments, one would expect a wide variance in the types of operations that U.S. forces might be called on to conduct in these countries. Nevertheless, it is possible to define a general strategy for military operations against terrorist and insurgent groups. Since the goal in all cases is to help create or enhance stability in key areas abroad

---

[2]   This monograph focuses on military capabilities with the intent of contributing to ongoing deliberations within the Department of Defense (DoD). However, dealing with the challenges of the post post–Cold War world described in the last chapter is far from exclusively a DoD problem. Serious attention must be paid to the organization and roles of all U.S. government agencies whose resources will be essential to implement a new, ambitious grand strategy. Such attention must focus not just on the Washington interagency process but also on field implementation and the "country team" approach. U.S. grand strategy will not succeed if it views the strategic landscape solely through a military lens and acts accordingly.

[3]   For states that that can effectively police their populations and that seek to eradicate terrorist groups, intelligence sharing, coordination of legal practices, and other policy instruments play leading roles. For states that resist pressures to act against terrorist groups within their jurisdictions, classic instruments of coercion and persuasion remain appropriate.

so that governments can effectively control their own territories, we refer to these efforts as *stability operations.*

Conceptually, U.S. stability operations can be categorized by the military role the U.S. armed forces are playing. The U.S. role may be direct, indirect, or a combination thereof. In direct stability operations, U.S. forces conduct direct (and perhaps unilateral) combat operations against insurgents, terrorists, and other subversive elements. In indirect stability operations, U.S. forces support indigenous government operations against subversive elements. Between these two poles are many gradations that mix direct and indirect operations.

Normally, the United States will want to operate against foreign terrorist and insurgent threats as indirectly as possible. Whatever the U.S. role, the mission of these operations is to eliminate or neutralize terrorist and insurgent groups threatening U.S. interests. Operations in support of this mission will generally be undertaken in cooperation with (and, indeed, in support of) forces of the host country. The armed forces of the United States lack the manpower and resources to conduct direct stability operations in all the countries in the world where threatening groups exist. But even if they could undertake direct operations on such a scale, lasting success is more likely to result when the forces prosecuting operations in the field are from the host country. If they are disciplined and well trained, local forces are far less likely to engender feelings of resentment within the populace than are forces of an outside power. Local forces are also often better positioned than foreigners to develop accurate intelligence about groups operating within their borders. Ultimately, defeating terrorist and insurgent groups is about bringing security and good governance to the populations in which subversive groups would seek to operate. When that happens, the popular support on which such groups depend for survival dries up. Training; equipping; advising; and, as appropriate, assisting host-country forces, then, are the sine qua non of effective campaigns against terrorist and insurgent groups.

Specific campaigns will generally comprise different combinations of the following operational objectives:

- strengthening the capabilities and will of host government forces

- disrupting the activities of terrorists and insurgents
- helping to alienate terrorists and insurgents from the populace
- finding and capturing or killing terrorists
- gathering intelligence about terrorist networks and activities around the world
- protecting friendly forces and bases.[4]

If this vision of future U.S. military operations against terrorist groups and insurgents is an accurate guide to strategy, it suggests that the widely used term *war on terrorism* is unfortunate. The sorts of operations envisaged here are likely to be long-term efforts in which the actual use of force, at least by U.S. military personnel, is only sporadic. Indeed, military operations against terrorist groups will have much in common with effective counterinsurgency operations if they are to be successful. Accordingly, the hallmarks of effective counterterrorist efforts generally will be that

- the host government, not the United States, plays the leading role in hunting down the terrorists
- the terrorists are subjected to relentless pressure and are not able to determine the tempo and timing of operations but rather are forced to react to government-initiated operations
- operations are "information intensive," depending crucially on accurate information on terrorists' activities, location, and identities
- most importantly, the host government must win the loyalty of its populace, alienating the terrorists from potential sources of support.

These considerations point to a demanding set of operating environments for U.S. forces charged with countering terrorist groups abroad. These forces will be called on to forge strong relationships with host-country personnel, to show great discretion conducting opera-

---

[4] For more on strategies for countering terrorist and insurgent groups and their implications for DoD, see Ochmanek (2003), on which this section is based.

tions, to maintain a low profile in the host country, yet to be able to react swiftly and effectively when promising targets arise.

Forces and assets relevant to these missions tend to be in chronically short supply within DoD. They include the following:

- conventional and SOF trained to operate effectively in foreign settings
- surveillance platforms and operators, human intelligence specialists, and imagery and intelligence analysts
- military police and other force-protection assets
- base operating support personnel and equipment to provide vital functions, such as communications, housing, and transportation, at a wide range of operating locations
- combat search and rescue (for U.S. and host-country personnel), as well as SOF insertion and extraction capabilities
- people and equipment to deliver humanitarian services, including engineers, doctors and dentists, public health specialists, tactical airlift aircraft, and crews.

Supporting New Democracies

A consensus appears to be growing that, in countries where important U.S. interests are engaged, the nation has a stake in preventing elements hostile to these interests from sowing unrest and using violence to prevent the establishment of stable institutions of democratic governance. At times, this may require the U.S. armed forces to conduct direct stability operations as a component of broader U.S. "nation-building."

While DoD does not by any means have a monopoly on instruments for such missions, U.S. military forces play important roles in them. Given the nation's focus on expanding democracy, DoD will need to take steps to ensure that it fields forces capable of undertaking effective direct stability operations on a very significant scale and for many years to come. What will these missions likely entail? Our operations in Iraq since the fall of Saddam Hussein's regime and, especially, in Afghanistan since the fall of the Taliban provide insights. In general, the primary objectives of U.S. forces are to provide a secure external and internal environment so that political, economic, and social development may proceed. The immediate end state toward which U.S. forces work is to get the country to reach a point at which the U.S. role reverts to that of advisory assistance and training, as outlined in the previous section. Once this threshold is reached, U.S. forces can take on a much lower internal profile, reducing the potential to become a lightning rod for criticism and a rallying point for forces opposed to the central government. Reaching that point may be difficult, however. Moreover, even when such a point has been reached, the presence of outside forces may be necessary to establish a regional security environment that permits friendly governments to focus their resources on internal development.

The U.S. experience in Iraq following the elimination of Saddam Hussein's regime is a cautionary example: Nation-building is hard, costly, and time consuming under the best of circumstances. Its inherent difficulties are compounded when a society is wracked by conflict. While the importance of democratic reform as a means of countering the spread of extremist ideologies is well recognized, the United States and its allies will have to be selective and judicious in deciding how best to allocate their resources to these efforts.

Depending on the state of the host government and society, U.S. and other outside forces may need to conduct the following types of operations:

- providing security for key facilities and population centers
- in the immediate aftermath of conflict, providing for governance of the state
- developing intelligence on the identity and the modus operandi of antigovernment elements
- monitoring borders and interdicting the flow of fighters, weapons, and material support into and out of the country
- arresting or, if necessary, killing those who employ or advocate violence against the government and security forces
- organizing, recruiting, training, equipping, and assisting security forces for the country

- helping the new government win the loyalty of its people by providing information about government policies and by offering humanitarian resources, infrastructure development, and other incentives to communities that support the government.[5]

Importantly, in their training and assistance efforts, U.S. and other Western forces do more than simply impart military skills. They also seek, directly and indirectly, to inculcate in their counterparts an understanding of and appreciation for democratic values, including the rule of law and civilian control over military institutions.

The forces and capabilities required for these sorts of operations are essentially the same as those required for countering terrorist and insurgent groups. Depending on the balance of power between the government and the forces of disorder, fairly large increments of outside combat forces might also be required. Clearly, if the United States is to sustain a level of effort in these mission areas commensurate with the nation's interest in defeating terrorism and establishing democracy, changes will be required in how U.S. ground forces are organized, trained, and prepared for rotations abroad.[6]

Deterring and Defeating Regional Adversaries

Key dynamics in the international arena coupled with the U.S. response to them have pushed to the fore "new" missions of countering terrorist and insurgent groups and helping to stabilize conditions in newly democratic states. But more-familiar missions remain and are, in many ways, as important as ever. And, as the brief review of emerging threats in Chapter Two strongly suggests, these missions are growing significantly more demanding.

For example, both North Korea and Iran pose significantly greater military challenges than did Iraq or, certainly, Serbia. In Iran's case,

---

[5] For a more thorough review of strategies for postconflict stability operations, see Dobbins et al. (2003).

[6] Whittle (2005).

there is the problem of scale: Iran is approximately three times larger than Iraq and has roughly three times the population. If even a sizable minority of its people opposed the notion of being invaded and occupied by the United States, the U.S. forces would simply lack the capacity to occupy and pacify the nation. In addition, both Iran and North Korea have at their disposal military capabilities that were not present to a significant degree in Iraq's armed forces. For instance, they have a panoply of means, including submarines, mines, antiship cruise missiles, and SOF, for attacking naval forces and merchant shipping. Iran is also projected to field much-more-capable surface-to-air missile (SAM) systems than either Iraq or Serbia possessed. And both Iran and North Korea are believed to possess chemical and biological weapons. Of course, North Korea is believed to have tested a nuclear device and is working to develop a nuclear arsenal. Iran appears to be working covertly toward the same goal. If mated to survivable long-range delivery systems, such as the mobile missile systems that both countries have deployed, even a modest number of these weapons (say, ten to twelve) would radically alter the military situation in the region. Unless enemy leaders can somehow be deterred from using nuclear weapons, forward bases and concentrations of troops or materiel on land may become untenable. Further, regional allies may be unwilling to participate in coalition operations against a nuclear armed power or to permit U.S. forces to base there for fear of being attacked. Obviously, deterrence of nuclear use becomes problematic if the goal of a U.S.-led military operation is to end the regime of the adversary state. What appears at first to be a familiar mission of regional power projection is taking on new and troubling dimensions.

Chapter Five addresses the implications of these trends for modernization priorities, but we list here the primary types of forces and capabilities called for in prosecuting operations against regional adversaries:

- large numbers of ships and cargo aircraft to transport forces to the theater and to support sustained operations

- aerial refueling assets to support the airlift effort and to allow surveillance and combat aircraft to operate effectively, especially if bases outside the theater are used
- air and missile defenses to protect forward forces and bases and to extend some measure of protection to allies' civil infrastructure and populations
- airborne and space-based platforms to provide comprehensive surveillance over enemy territory
- capabilities for gaining and maintaining air and maritime superiority over and around the enemy's territory so that joint forces can observe and strike enemy forces at will and enjoy freedom of maneuver
- aircraft and cruise missiles for responsive; precise; and, at times, high-volume attacks on enemy forces and supporting infrastructure.

The types of forces and capabilities listed above would be required in almost any large-scale military operation against a capable regional adversary, such as Iran or North Korea, whether the chief purpose of that operation was to coerce the opposing regime into changing its policies, to deny it certain military capabilities, or to protect regional allies and forces from attacks by enemy forces. Ground forces and amphibious forces, perhaps in sizable numbers, would also be required for some campaigns, particularly if their objective was to take down the enemy regime and occupy the country. Campaigns with more-limited objectives—for instance, preventing North Korean forces from shelling Seoul and environs with long-range artillery or coercing Iran's leaders by embargoing that country's oil exports—might also call for ground and/or amphibious operations to seize and hold portions of the country. But it is also possible to imagine operations, particularly against Iran, that feature little or no commitment of U.S. ground forces.

Dissuading Military Competition in Asia

China was not mentioned in the section above because, although it may become a military adversary, China stands apart from other states both qualitatively and quantitatively and poses distinct military and strategic challenges.[7] This is not just because China is one or more orders of magnitude larger and richer than states like North Korea and Iran. It is also because the political dynamics between China and the rest of the world are different from those characterized by what used to be termed "rogue states." By all indications, China is ruled by a fairly risk-averse set of leaders who seem, at least for the present, to be largely satisfied with the international system and its norms. To be sure, China aspires to carry more geostrategic weight, commensurate with its growing political and economic reach, but these ambitions are, at least in theory, compatible with a peaceful order in Asia. In fact, other than the issue of Taiwan's future status, and absent some uncharacteristically reckless behavior by China's rulers, it is difficult to imagine plausible circumstances that could bring the United States and its allies into large-scale military conflict with China. For these reasons, and because the issue of Taiwan per se does not impinge on the survival interests of either side, should conflict occur, deterrence of nuclear attacks on the American and Chinese homelands should be fairly robust.[8]

Comparing this situation with the real possibility of nuclear use in conflicts involving lesser regional powers, one may be tempted to conclude that the military requirements associated with deterring conflict and dissuading military competition with China might be relatively easy. This would be a mistake. China, which is already among

---

[7] Other large and technically advanced states, such as Russia and, in the future, India, could pose operational challenges similar to those discussed here. However, neither of these countries seems likely to pursue objectives and policies that would plausibly lead to large-scale military conflict with the United States.

[8] An important exception, which cannot easily be dismissed, would be the perception on the part of China's leaders that a failure to achieve its goals should war commence in the Taiwan Strait would be likely to lead to the fall of the Chinese Communist Party. In this context, it is possible to imagine China's leaders resorting to risky or provocative military options.

the world's top spenders on military forces, is expanding its military budgets at double-digit rates every year. And the Chinese are focusing their modernization efforts on precisely the sorts of capabilities designed to thwart U.S. power-projection operations. For example,

- China has fielded large numbers of theater ballistic missiles (TBMs) and has been improving their accuracy. Soon, the Chinese will be in a position to destroy specific elements of targeted military facilities, such as runways, taxiways, fuel storage tanks, and living quarters on air bases, or supply ships at quayside, loading facilities, and marshalling yards at ports. Compounding this threat, the Chinese are also developing modern cruise missiles.
- The Chinese are fielding a modern, integrated air defense system with large numbers of highly capable long-range SAMs. Within this decade, the PLA Air Force will have the world's second or third largest fleet of advanced, fourth-generation fighter aircraft.
- China is investing in a panoply of advanced systems for attacking surface ships, including quiet submarines, air- and sea-launched antiship cruise missiles, long-range aircraft and sensors, and modern surface combatants.
- The Chinese are increasing the number and sophistication of their military satellites, even as they also test means for interfering with the satellites of other nations.[9]

Projecting power into East Asia to defeat possible Chinese aggression will be by far the most difficult challenge U.S. forces would face in a conventional conflict. Accordingly, the mission of deterring China and dissuading military competition in East Asia will serve as the prime force motivating the modernization of the Air Force and Navy. As with defeating regional aggressors, it is of paramount importance that DoD improve its ability to defeat attacks by ballistic missiles. To thwart Chinese military options, it will be necessary to protect not only forces and bases but also Taiwan's people and infrastructure from

---

[9] For an overview of key aspects of a hypothetical conflict over Taiwan, see Shlapak, Orletsky, and Wilson (2000), especially pp. 54–57, which focus on implications of China's acquisition of more modern conventional weapons.

missile attack. Other capabilities required to effectively counter a Chinese offensive would be broadly similar to those highlighted above for defeating regional adversaries. But the timelines associated with engaging Chinese forces may be very short: U.S. forces might have only a few days (or less) in which to mobilize and deploy to the region before the shooting begins. This places a premium on forces that can deploy quickly and that have large margins of qualitative superiority over the enemy.[10] In addition to blunting missile attacks, it will be particularly important that U.S. forces be able rapidly to defeat Chinese air attacks, break down China's integrated air defenses (fighters, long-range SAMs, and command-and-control systems) deployed near the coast, and interdict enemy naval vessels operating in and near the Taiwan Strait. These requirements argue for significant forward basing of key U.S. capabilities, configured in such a way as to minimize their vulnerability to preemptive attack.

Defending the Homeland

Protecting the nation from attack is a fundamental responsibility of any government. DoD's primary contribution to this core objective is to identify and defeat threats abroad, be they in the form of conventional military forces or terrorist groups, before they reach U.S. shores. In this regard, protecting the nation from attacks by small numbers of long-range ballistic missiles—a threat that could emerge over the next decade—has gained new emphasis. Thought is also being given to options for defending against cruise missile attacks that could be launched from naval combatants or from converted merchant ships off the coasts. Since September 11, 2001, the Air Force has also been tasked with providing some capability to intercept and shoot down civil aircraft that have been commandeered by terrorists before these aircraft can be used as weapons. Given the attackers' ability to choose

---

[10] Lanchester's square law teaches us that quantity has a quality all its own. If a force half the size of its opponent is to fight to a draw, it must be four times as capable on a unit-for-unit basis. If U.S. forces are to fight the opening engagements of a conflict outnumbered, they must be far superior qualitatively to prevail.

the time and place for such attacks, it is not feasible to provide comprehensive protection against such threats by posturing fighter, tanker, and Airborne Warning and Control System aircraft across the nation. Rather, measures to make it far more difficult to commandeer aircraft, such as passenger screening, strengthening cockpit doors, and putting air marshals on board most flights, offer much higher payoff.

In pursuing their primary missions, the U.S. armed forces field certain capabilities that can supplement those of other agencies charged with monitoring, screening, and intercepting threats at the borders, such as the Coast Guard, the Immigration and Naturalization Service, and the Customs Service. Perhaps the most often used of these capabilities is aerial surveillance of maritime and land approaches to the United States. Other DoD assets, including airlift and surveillance aircraft, and decontamination assets, may be useful in responding to potential attacks. U.S. ground forces—perhaps in substantial numbers—might also be called on to help restore civil order after a massive attack or a major natural disaster. However, aside from forces that defend the country against air and missile attacks, the command-and-control functions associated with homeland defense, and the possibility that some forces—largely ground forces—may need to be withheld to deal with the consequences of a catastrophic attack on the United States, this mission is not an overriding factor in sizing and shaping the armed forces.

Countering the Proliferation of Nuclear Weapons

The imperative of countering the spread of nuclear weapons cuts across several of the missions discussed here. Because of the vast destructive potential of these weapons, DoD and other agencies of the U.S. government must do everything possible to monitor existing arsenals in hostile countries, as well as potential sources of nuclear technologies and fissile materials. Preventing enemies from getting access to or using nuclear weapons will also be a part of military operations before, during, and after combat.

One of the nightmare scenarios associated with nuclear weapons merits special mention: The problem of "loose nukes" in a failing state. A number of permutations of this scenario are imaginable, but at its core, it involves the possible loss of control over all or part of an arsenal of nuclear weapons by a government that has become unable to control some or all of its territory. If it were thought that a faction contending for control of the country might use or disperse the weapons, U.S. leaders would have to consider employing military forces in an attempt to secure or neutralize them. It goes without saying that the difficulties and risks associated with such an operation would be legion. They would include determining where the weapons are; the level of security at the facilities and in the surrounding areas; which forces within the country, if any, might be sympathetic to efforts to secure the weapons; which would be hostile; and so forth. One cannot expect this sort of operation to be executed successfully without extensive planning and training. If U.S. leaders wish to guard against failure under such circumstances, appropriate preparations must be made well in advance. These considerations have implications for DoD's deliberate planning process; its intelligence collection and analysis efforts; and for training, equipping, and posturing elements of the forces. Capabilities that would be especially useful include the following:

- sources of human intelligence in regional states that have fielded nuclear weapons
- the ability to detect and track fissile material and activities related to the fabrication of nuclear weapons using remote sensors
- the ability to insert SOF or infantry forces deep into contested territory and to support them with information, firepower, and supplies once they are deployed
- the ability to deny personnel access to a defined area for periods of hours to days.

Although such a mission would be relatively small in terms of forces, specialized equipment will be needed to detect, track, and deny hostile possession of nuclear weapons.

Setting Aggregate Levels of Capability

Until this point, we have focused on the qualitative dimension of force planning: What types of capabilities should our armed forces possess to accomplish the most important missions assigned to them? Defense planning and resource allocation must also be informed by an appreciation of the quantitative dimension: How much aggregate capability is appropriate? During the first decade after the Cold War, U.S. general-purpose forces were sized primarily by the requirement to be able to fight and win two major regional conflicts "in overlapping time frames." While it was recognized that missions other than defeating regional aggressor states would require some specialized capabilities, these missions were treated essentially as lesser included cases for sizing the overall force. The defense strategy promulgated in 2001 posited a more-elaborate criterion for sizing the force. DoD has stated that U.S. forces should be able to

- defend the United States
- deter aggression and coercion forward in four critical regions[11]
- swiftly defeat aggression in overlapping major conflicts while preserving the option to call for a decisive victory in one of them, including the possibility of regime change and occupation
- conduct a limited number of smaller-scale contingency operations.[12]

The force sizing construct outlined in Quadrennial Defense Review (QDR) 2001 came to be known as "1-4-2-1." Although it emphasized a wider range of challenges than captured previously, it did not account for the challenges faced today in defeating terrorists and insurgents abroad. Moreover, as outlined previously, this approach does not capture the likely long-term requirements associated with promoting democracy and freedom abroad, a likely mainstay of U.S. strategy.

---

[11] The four regions are Europe, Northeast Asia, the East Asian littoral, and the Middle East and Southwest Asia.

[12] DoD (2001, p. 17).

For these reasons, we conclude that the "1-4-2-1" criterion no longer comports well with the actual requirements of U.S. strategy.[13] Nor need it apply equally to all of the military services; hence the need for a new division of labor among them. *What follows is a suggested new approach, which both reflects the demands of U.S. grand strategy and the difficult military challenges U.S. forces will confront in the years to come.*

One Homeland

It is appropriate to begin the force sizing requirement with "1," if only as a reminder of the centrality of protecting the territory and people of the United States from attack. But in practical terms, within DoD, only capabilities for the defense of the nation from air and missile attack are actually sized by this requirement. Other capabilities that the armed forces might contribute to defending the homeland or to mitigating the consequences of an attack exist because they were fielded to undertake other missions.

With this, however, comes one critically important caution: Should the United States experience an attack that is of a scale much larger than the attacks of September 11, 2001, significant portions of the U.S. armed forces, particularly the Army (active duty units and National Guard), could be involved in operations within the United States aimed at helping to manage and remediate the consequences of such an attack, while working to avert potential follow-up attacks. And DoD may still want to establish a *withhold*—some number of forces to be held in reserve in the United States—to contend with the consequences of a catastrophic attack. Depending on the size of attack (or attacks) envisioned, a withhold could involve substantial numbers of forces.

---

[13] DoD came to a similar conclusion in its QDR of 2005–2006. Specifically, the leadership of the department recognized that, to make headway against terrorist groups abroad, U.S. forces will need to be engaged in a number of "long-duration operations, including unconventional warfare, foreign internal defense, counterterrorism, counterinsurgency, and stabilization and reconstruction operations." It has also recognized that such operations would, perforce, be conducted "around the globe and not only in and from the four regions called out in the 2001 QDR" (see DoD, 2006, p. 36).

Beyond Four Regions

The era is gone when strategists could divide the planet into regions where the nation has important interests at stake (e.g., trade relationships, access to critical resources, alliance commitments) and where it does not. In terms of classic geopolitics, Afghanistan and Sudan were beyond the strategic purview of the United States, yet they were the breeding grounds of al Qaeda. In a world in which small groups of individuals can acquire the means to kill thousands, the United States and its security partners cannot be indifferent to conditions in any other state if a terrorist group with the intent and capability to attack them might be gestating there. This is why the United States today deploys roughly 15,000 troops in Afghanistan. It is also why, since 2001, U.S. forces have been actively engaged in training and advisory assistance missions in such places as Georgia, the Horn of Africa, and the Sahel, as well as other areas that lie outside of the four regions highlighted in the defense strategy of 2001. The actual number of regions in which U.S. forces should expect to conduct direct and indirect stability operations, then, is indeterminate but is certainly larger than four. In fact, it is not useful to characterize the demand for forces to conduct these operations in terms of "regions." Today, large portions of the force structure are engaged in Iraq and Afghanistan. In a few years, deployment levels and the distribution of forces will almost certainly be quite different.

Rather than fixating on some number of regions—which will, unavoidably, be wrong—DoD should consider committing a sizable increment of force structure to these missions and plan to employ it (at a sustainable pace) in executing them.[14] If a placeholder is needed for the number of ongoing missions of this type and for classical deterrence and assurance missions, the number is "n." As discussed above, we do not envision the "Phase IV" operations in Iraq as the template for these types of missions. Whenever possible, the number of outside

---

[14] As we argue in Chapter Five, if U.S. forces were to undertake indirect stability operations in countries facing active or latent Islamist insurgencies, along with similar missions in selected countries coping with non-Islamist internal challenges (e.g., Colombia), they would find themselves engaged, in substantial numbers and on a sustained basis, in approximately 50 countries scattered across Eurasia, Africa, and Latin America.

forces involved should be small, and the lion's share of the actual in-the-field operations should be undertaken by host-country forces.

Nevertheless, *in aggregate*, missions to train and advise local forces and to help new regimes bring stability to their countries along with democratic governance are typically labor intensive. They call for U.S. forces to be present on the ground, sometimes in substantial numbers, working closely with host-country forces and, in some cases, conducting operations against terrorists and insurgents. If the United States and its allies are to defeat or maintain pressure on the terrorist and insurgent groups that pose the greatest threats to their interests, a substantial level of effort will be required, and it will have to be sustained over many years, irrespective of the future course of events in Iraq and Afghanistan. In fact, these missions should become a primary factor in sizing the Army and Marine Corps, as well as SOF.

Two Major Combat Operations
The rationale behind fielding forces sufficient to prevail in two wars is sound and has been a basis for U.S. planning for more than 50 years.[15] Because the United States has important interests and alliances in multiple regions of the world and because plausible military threats to these interests exist in more than one region, we must avoid placing ourselves in a situation in which we could neither deter nor defend against aggression, even when substantial U.S. forces are engaged in conflict. Adopting something less than a "two war" criterion for sizing U.S. forces might also cause important allies to question the value of their security partnerships with the United States, leading to the unraveling of alliances and a loss of American influence. But the persistence of the number "2" in the force sizing criterion does not imply stasis in the composition of the forces called for to fight and win wars. As we have seen, the challenges that regional adversaries and China pose are changing dramatically. U.S. forces engaging in hostilities against such foes must find ways to deal with a host of threats to naval forces; modern air defenses; chemical and biological weapons; and, most wor-

---

[15] Since the time of the Korean War, U.S. planners have sought to field forces capable of winning overlapping, if not simultaneous, wars in Europe and Asia.

risome, ballistic missiles and nuclear weapons. Defeating or blunting these threats will require extensive and costly modernization efforts. We suggest below that the requirement to project power against two regional adversaries should remain relevant to determining the overall size and shape of the U.S. Navy and Air Force.

One "Decisive Win" and Occupation

U.S. leaders will want to maintain the capability to defeat the forces of a regional adversary comprehensively, to occupy the country, and to forcibly remove its regime from power. If and as regional adversaries acquire "strategic deterrent" forces, pursuing such objectives via overt military means may become less and less feasible. But having the potential to invade and occupy an enemy's country and take down its leadership is a powerful trump card that should be maintained.[16]

Implications for Forces and Posture

What this all means for the overall size and shape of the armed forces is, to a first order, fairly clear: The Army and Marine Corps, along with much of the special operations community, must play the leading roles in countering terrorist and insurgent groups abroad and in helping to stabilize nations trying to emerge from authoritarian forms of governance. The key to long-term success in these operations is to foster the emergence of competent security forces within host countries so that governments that share the U.S. interest in suppressing terrorism and insurgency can do so increasingly on their own. The host-country forces that accomplish these missions will be primarily ground forces and will, perforce, be trained and assisted by other ground forces. U.S. naval and air forces can contribute important capabilities, but they will generally play supporting roles.

The Army must also maintain the capability, working with its joint partners, to deliver decisive victory against a regional adversary.

---

[16] For an assessment of the efficacy of military operations to remove enemy leaders and of the operational challenges associated with such missions, see Hosmer (2001).

This will require the Army to master two distinct "primary" mission areas, conventional warfighting and stability operations.

Both the Navy and Air Force, by contrast, must remain focused on conducting large-scale power-projection operations against the forces of other nations as their primary raison d'être. These two services already possess the nation's primary means for projecting military power swiftly across long distances and for striking at the enemy's centers of gravity. U.S. concepts of operation for all three of the major combat scenarios we regard as plausible—Korea, China-Taiwan, and Iran—call for large-scale air and naval forces to defeat enemy thrusts, gain freedom to operate on and near the enemy's territory, and destroy the enemy's capacity to make war. And U.S. forces conducting both stability operations and large-scale combat will want more-comprehensive and more-accurate information about the enemy—a requirement that will place greater demands on air, naval, and space forces.

Because of the crucial importance of the counterterror and stabilization missions, and because of the changing nature of the threat that regional adversaries posed, *the Army and Marine Corps reasonably could be relieved of the requirement of preparing forces to fight in the second of two nearly simultaneous wars.* Our concept for defending Taiwan does not call for substantial numbers of U.S. ground forces. And in RAND Corporation war games featuring conflict with Iran, we do not identify substantial roles for ground and amphibious forces.[17] Even North Korea, which has long posed a serious threat of armored invasion across the demilitarized zone, is evolving into a more-complex problem, in which the focused application of naval and air forces in support of improving South Korean capabilities could reduce the demand for U.S. ground forces early in a conflict.[18] Of course, the pos-

---

[17] Iran's capabilities for invading its neighbors with mechanized ground forces are not impressive. The primary uses for U.S. ground and amphibious forces in scenarios involving conflict with Iran center on seizing and holding, for limited periods, relatively small portions of territory for coercive purposes or to preclude certain Iranian military options.

[18] A rational North Korean leadership must realize that an invasion of South Korea would be suicide if conducted only with conventional forces. Accordingly, more-interesting conflict scenarios for U.S. and Republic of Korea planners involve efforts to develop coercive or denial strategies aimed at neutralizing Pyongyang's nuclear weapon capabilities.

sibility will always remain that the United States could be confronted by a war that it failed to foresee. Alternatively, scenarios involving Iran, North Korea, and China might evolve unpredictably. As a result, it will remain imperative that U.S. ground forces maintain superior capabilities for conventional operations. Given the competing demands of the new grand strategy, however, it will be sensible to size these capabilities to conduct a single major regional conflict at any given time.

Transitioning the Army and Marine Corps to "one war" forces does not imply that troop numbers or the force structure of either service should decline. Such a transition would, however, make it possible for large portions of the two ground-oriented services to focus increasingly on preparing for and carrying out the vital missions of countering terrorist groups and helping to stabilize emerging democracies. Chapter Five offers ideas for how each service's efforts might be modified to better support the demands described here.

Finally, to contend with the sorts of challenges we envisage, the United States will wish to change substantially the posture of its forces and bases overseas. Although stationing and deploying U.S. forces in certain areas overseas can carry political and psychological value in and of itself, important elements of current overseas presence lack a strong operational or strategic rationale,[19] and this will ultimately undermine their political utility. Moreover, some U.S. overseas forces and bases are militarily vulnerable today and are likely to become more vulnerable in the future. If these vulnerabilities are not corrected, their strategic and operational utility will be dubious and potentially dangerous if the deployments invite preemptive attack. And just as the defense strategy will require more differentiated roles for U.S. military forces, so too will the United States need to maintain more diverse and differentiated forms of presence and basing overseas.

In Europe, the United States should move beyond the "heavy" footprint of permanently based forces it maintains in Germany and

---

[19] For example, the presence of heavy ground forces in Europe provides little value to the defense of Europe, which is no longer threatened by a Soviet invasion. The argument that heavy ground forces in Europe are easier to deploy to potential trouble spots rests on the dubious assumption that these forces can be readily moved to the south over the Alps to Mediterranean ports.

develop instead an expeditionary posture that is better suited to training with allies away from garrison and bringing military assistance to new allies and partners in Eastern and Southeastern Europe, the Caucasus, and Africa.[20] Current plans to return heavy Army forces to the United States should proceed apace, as should the deployment of one of the Army's medium-weight Stryker brigades to Europe. For its part, Air Force should be more aggressive in exploring the feasibility of establishing a more-expeditionary presence—and perhaps even permanent basing—closer to potential operating areas in the Middle East and the Caucasus. The Navy can maintain an in-transit carrier presence but may need to consider more missile defense cooperation with NATO countries, which, in turn, may require more surface combatant presence in the Mediterranean. SOF can stage effectively from Southern Europe if a suitable home can be found there for them. If not, U.S. SOF in Europe could be returned to the United States and be deployed rotationally to Africa, the Caucasus, the Middle East, and elsewhere.

The wars in Afghanistan and Iraq will profoundly affect the U.S. military presence in the Middle East and in South and Central Asia. Existing infrastructure in the Persian Gulf region is largely a reflection of U.S. efforts through the 1990s to contain and ultimately defeat Iraqi aggression. While the United States ultimately will want to maintain a long-term military presence in the Middle East and South and Central Asia, it is not clear that all existing military infrastructure is appropriate or will be required for future missions. In general, therefore, additional investments in Persian Gulf infrastructure should await further resolution of the situations in Afghanistan and, particularly, Iraq, as well as clarification of broader U.S. strategic objectives. One matter, however, is clear: Air bases in the Gulf region that might be used by deploying U.S. forces will need to be hardened against attacks by ballistic and cruise missiles if the United States is to retain a credible power-projection capability vis-à-vis Iran. Even fairly inaccurate missiles, if

---

[20] The importance of such training should not be forgotten. NATO operates as an Allied force in Afghanistan today, while the European Union has relieved NATO and U.S. forces in the Balkans. These developments are possible because of decades of U.S.-led combined training and operations. One approach to supporting expeditionary forces worldwide can be found in Killingsworth et al. (2000).

armed with unguided submunitions, can achieve a high probability of kill against "soft" targets, such as aircraft in the open, above-ground fuel storage tanks, and personnel bivouacked in tents.[21]

Temporary infrastructure in Iraq and Afghanistan may or may not form the basis for a longer-term presence in these countries. But U.S. military planners should not rule out the possibility that both countries might seek some form of long-term security relationship with the United States and would perhaps welcome a modest presence of U.S. military forces. Similarly, planners should examine the possibility that one or both countries might invite U.S. forces to leave, perhaps on an expedited basis. In either case, the complexion of the U.S. force presence in the Middle East and South Asia will change fundamentally in the next several years.

The prospects of Korean nuclear weapons and China's military emergence in Asia will greatly affect U.S. military relationships in Asia and the U.S. military posture in the region. So, too, will the presence of Islamic extremism in Southeast Asia. Indeed, Asia is the one region where the full set of challenges identified in Chapter Two—terrorism, nuclear proliferation, and growing Chinese military power—overlap. Existing military facilities in Asia are becoming increasingly vulnerable, and the U.S. ability to reinforce quickly with air and naval forces from beyond the region is not adequate to counter the growing threat. Area missile defense appears to be a major gap in existing capabilities. The United States lacks sufficient infrastructure and training and advisory relationships in Southeast Asia to assist local nations in countering Islamic extremism. The United States needs to work with its Asian partners to develop additional basing infrastructure in such places as the Ryukyu Islands, the Philippine Islands, Singapore, and Thailand. The U.S. Navy and Air Force should consider conducting additional routine air and naval training and operations in the western Pacific. The Army and Marine Corps, in conjunction with SOF, should expand the scope and duration of advisory and assistance missions throughout Southeast Asia. The United States should at the same

---

[21] For an overview of the threats posed by ballistic and cruise missiles to forward-deployed air forces, see Stillion and Orletsky (1999, pp. 78–80).

time take steps to improve its ability to deploy combat forces quickly to the region. To conduct rapid and robust power-projection operations into East Asia, U.S. naval forces in the Pacific will have to continue to shift their "center of mass" westward. The goal should be a capability to respond to threats or provocations in days—not weeks.

In general, this will mean increasing the number and capabilities of assets typically deployed in Hawaii, Guam, Japan, and Southeast Asia. Among other initiatives, the Air Force and Navy should continue to upgrade facilities on Guam and routinely deploy more power-projection assets there.[22] More attention also should be given to command-and-control arrangements, particularly given the potential for multiple military operations within the Pacific theater. And the United States needs to be forthcoming in working with its partners in Korea and Japan to remove unnecessary irritants so that the U.S. military presence in these areas remains viable over the longer term.

Finally, because the threats to the United States have become global and because we are not able to predict precisely where U.S. interests will be challenged, more attention needs to be given to understanding how U.S. forces will reach areas that have not been traditional loci for U.S. military operations. This places a premium on both strategic agility—the ability to move forces and assets quickly from place to place—and on global sustainment—the ability to support large numbers of geographically dispersed operations over prolonged periods. Broadly speaking, DoD's existing transportation infrastructure is well suited to moving people, equipment, and supplies east and west from the United States to various parts of the world. It is less well suited for supporting even modestly sized operations north and south, from North America to South America, from Europe to Africa, from the Caucasus and Central Asia to South Asia, or from Northeast Asia to Southeast Asia. More attention should be paid to creating the proper legal and support arrangements so that U.S. forces and supplies, including humanitarian assistance supplies, can be moved throughout the globe on short notice.

---

[22] See Khalilzad et al. (2001).

CHAPTER FOUR
What Will It Mean to Be Joint?

Coming out of the American experiences in World War II, defense reforms for more than half a century have sought to unify U.S. military planning, centralize the resource allocation process, create efficiencies in acquisition and support activities, and strengthen civilian control over military decisions. But most importantly, defense reforms have sought to create the conditions for greater military effectiveness.

The defense reforms immediately following World War II established the unified combatant commands. The reforms of 1958 took the military services out of the operational chain of command, in effect distinguishing between providers and users of forces—the military services as the providers and the unified commands as the users. And the Goldwater-Nichols reforms of 1986 clarified the operational chain of command and strengthened individual and institutional incentives to develop joint warfighting expertise. America's military proficiency since the 1986 reforms, particularly the ability of U.S. forces to achieve operational success on the battlefield, can be attributed in large measure to the decades-long efforts of those who understood that military power is most effective when all requisite elements of force can be brought to bear to achieve decisive results. In this regard, the long-elusive goal of joint operational prowess has been achieved.

But this same operational prowess could remain elusive in the face of the challenges outlined in this study. Moreover, operational prowess alone does not necessarily lead to joint tactical proficiency; neither does it guarantee strategic success.[1]

Different Demands for Joint Warfighting Prowess

As the preceding chapters have highlighted, American military forces will be called on to undertake an increasingly diverse set of missions. In some cases, this will lead to more sharply differentiated roles among the military services and supporting agencies. Not all forces can be optimized for the wide diversity of missions described here. The military services and supporting agencies must recognize that, in some instances, ground forces, for example, will absorb the preponderant share of responsibility for particular actions, while in other cases air and naval forces will provide the preponderance of capability. As Chapter Three highlights, the old notion of force building blocks,[2] in which each service had an expectation that it would be given a significant share of every major military task, must give way to a new concept of differentiated responsibilities, in which services and agencies refine old skills and develop new competencies to cover an expanding mission space without unnecessarily duplicating the contributions of others.

At the same time, some elements of this new set of missions will call for greater interdependence among the services and supporting agencies—not just operationally, but tactically. The relationship among air and ground forces, for example, will of necessity move beyond a set of supported and supporting relationships to tactical interdependence.[3] In many instances, it will no longer suffice for forces simply to "deconflict" their operations on the battlefield—that is, for forces to ensure that they are not working at cross-purposes or, worse, attacking each other. Rather, there will be many cases in which planning, training, and actual employment of forces will need to be fully integrated

---

[1] The views in this chapter are those of the authors. Several of the insights result from interviews with senior military leaders in 2003 and 2004.

[2] See, for example, the discussion in DoD (1993, pp. 13–26).

[3] For more on this point, see Chapter Five. See also Pirnie et al. (2005).

to achieve the desired battlefield effects. Ultimately, commanders will aspire to extend this level of tactical integration to operations with allied and coalition partners.

In short, additional time and attention will be required to achieve levels of joint warfighting prowess at the strategic and tactical levels of war similar to what exists today at the operational level.

Maintaining Strategic Focus

The missions described here—including countering terrorist and insurgent groups abroad, supporting emerging democracies, deterring and defeating regional adversaries, dissuading military competition in Asia, and helping to protect the U.S. homeland—require the long-term commitment of U.S. forces. They also will require a different level of attention from U.S. regional commanders. Given the complexity of the strategic environment and the high probability that multiple long- and short-term operations could be under way in a single theater of operations at any given time, regional commanders may well need to separate strategic and operational planning within their respective commands and devote a disproportionate amount of their personal time to maintaining strategic focus and securing strategic success.

Recent operational success has involved the deep commitment—indeed day-to-day, hour-to-hour involvement—of U.S. regional commanders. For example, it is interesting to observe that, in operations Desert Storm and Iraqi Freedom, Generals Norman Schwarzkopf and Tommy Franks essentially transitioned from being strategic commanders of all forces, activities, and relationships within their assigned regions to being field commanders, providing operational oversight—and at times tactical direction[4]—for the fighting taking place in one area of their assigned region. There is little doubt that the commitment of these field commanders led to the success of these operations. But it is also clear that, while these commanders were providing day-to-day direction and oversight in the field, they were less focused on

---

[4] See, for example, Franks (2004, pp. 491–492).

dealing with other pressing problems within their regions. Moreover, had events taken a different turn, and had they been challenged with multiple crises within their regions,[5] it is not clear that either of these commanders would have been well positioned to provide command oversight for all activities within his area of responsibility.

By contrast, during the run-up to and throughout Operation Enduring Freedom in Afghanistan, General Franks focused on developing coalition support; ensuring basing and throughput for coalition forces; working closely with Washington on postconflict governance and support alternatives; and, importantly, maintaining an effective deterrent posture elsewhere in the Central Command region. In a sense, the command model exercised in Operation Enduring Freedom may be a more appropriate example for future regional commanders than the models exercised in the two Gulf wars.

In short, the diverse challenges of this era might mean that theater commanders may no longer have the luxury of setting aside their duties of providing strategic direction for all forces, activities, and relationships within their regions to become field commanders for any single operation, large or small, within their areas of responsibility. The enormous demands of establishing, maintaining, and sustaining alliance and coalition relationships; the likelihood that multiple military operations could be under way in any single theater or area; and that ultimate strategic success will depend on winning the peace as well as the war mean that regional commanders must maintain a strategic perspective even as field commanders are directing combat operations. For these reasons—and somewhat ironically—we may need to see a return to World War II practices, in which theater commanders focused intensively on relationships with allies and partners, provided

---

[5] For example, had the first Gulf War escalated such that Israeli forces were committed directly in the fight, had weapons of mass destruction been used on the territory of other coalition partners, or had another crisis broken out in the Central Command area, it is not clear General Schwarzkopf would have been well positioned to provide strategic direction within his area of responsibility. Similarly, had events in the greater Middle East during the opening weeks of Operation Iraqi Freedom transpired such that there were urgent military needs in Afghanistan or, say, Pakistan—and recognizing that the Central Command staff was split between Tampa, Florida, and Qatar—it is not clear that General Franks would have been well positioned to provide command of his entire geographic theater.

broad direction for ongoing operations, and planned for future phases of the campaign. Day-to-day control of the actual fighting that took place in World War II was left largely to the field commanders—in today's parlance, the joint task force (JTF) commander.

If a new set of relationships within the regional command structure is to succeed, more time and attention need to be devoted to developing, training, and supporting the JTF commander. Just as it would be a mistake to assume that organizing, training, and equipping forces can be done on the fly, so, too, would it be a mistake to assume that the planning responsibilities and command-and-control functions of JTF commanders can be done without careful and continuous preparation.

Efforts that are under way within U.S. Joint Forces Command (USJFCOM) offer a promising start but, as currently constructed, may not lead to a satisfactory result. Without much closer collaboration among USJFCOM and the other regional and global commands on meeting the needs for future JTF commanders, it is likely that joint operational command and control will suffer the same inattention it has in the past. Existing "three-star" headquarters within the service component headquarters should form the basis for this effort. Finally, without robust mechanisms, procedures, and training to prepare future JTF commanders in joint operational command and control, regional commanders will continue to be tempted to assume field command when U.S. forces are committed to combat.

Achieving Joint Tactical Proficiency

Although the lessons of recent conflicts highlight operational proficiency, the lessons also note that this proficiency does not necessarily extend to tactical matters. Recent operations remain replete with incidents in which tactical commanders remained unaware of operational schemes of maneuver; existing joint and service doctrine inhibits tactical success on the battlefield; and, worse, the lack of tactical integration resulted in combat failures and unnecessary casualties.[6]

Part of the challenge can be explained by how joint forces currently are organized, fielded, and committed to combat. Regional commanders organize joint forces through service component commands; that is, every regional command has an Army, Navy, Air Force, Marine Corps, and SOF component. In planning operations, regional commands develop plans through their service components. Units are integrated at the component level, and the forces are supported through their parent services. Unless units have been assigned and collocated for training, there is no particular reason to assume at the time of any given operation that different service units have ever trained or operated together.

This joint tactical division of labor might be viable if service components had clearly defined battlefield roles. But as was highlighted previously and will be discussed in more detail in Chapter Five, we should assume greater, not less, interdependence among most elements of the force for a variety of missions. As American forces learned in Afghanistan, SOF, fighting alongside indigenous ground forces, became much more effective when they received supporting fire from naval- and land-based aircraft. Future Army ground-force operations will depend more and more on precision fire support from the air. Air and naval power projection will need to be increasingly integrated to effectively counter enemy antiaccess operations. And we believe greater effectiveness can be achieved by strengthening the relationship between the Marine Corps and SOF. In short, joint commanders and supporting services will need to facilitate more routine integration of tactical formations across a variety of military tasks.

To achieve new levels of joint tactical proficiency, JTF commanders will need to train units more routinely in joint operations. While service "centers of excellence," such as the Army's National Training

---

[6] See, for example, Johnson (forthcoming). Poor situational awareness during a chaotic fight combined with an absence of planning and inadequate identification, friend or foe capabilities resulted in the "friendly fire" deaths of several Marines in Nasiriyah on March 23, 2003, during OIF. See Second Marine Expeditionary Force (2003, pp. 11–14).

Center or Air Force's Fighter Weapons School, will remain an integral part of the training curriculum, additional effort must be given to attaining joint tactical proficiency. Just as the Goldwater-Nichols Act introduced incentives for capable officers to seek joint assignments, incentive structures for officer promotion at the O-5, -6, and -7 levels should also emphasize joint training. For example, the services should create incentive structures at the O-5, -6, and -7 levels to make seeking and exploiting joint training opportunities criteria for success in command positions. Forging these types of joint tactical arrangements—indeed, creating joint tactical interdependencies—and training and testing these arrangements routinely will be essential to support America's new grand strategy and confront the daunting challenges outlined in this report.

Moreover, if we are to assume that coalition operations will be the norm, additional time and attention will need to be given to integrating coalition members into various concepts of operation. This will, of necessity, need to become a focus of U.S. security cooperation activities.

A New Joint Division of Labor

Since the mid-1980s, the command and control of U.S. forces has been undergoing profound but underappreciated change. With the establishment of U.S. Space Command,[7] U.S. Transportation Command, and U.S. Special Operations Command (USSOCOM)—often referred to as functional commands—the U.S. command structure began a trend of consolidating and centralizing functions that has continued to this day.[8] This has created a new set of command-and-control arrangements for U.S. forces. In the past, there had been a rough division of labor between force providers (military services) and users (unified commands), but this new development has created a new

---

[7] In October 2002, U.S. Space Command merged with U.S. Strategic Command.

[8] Similar consolidation has taken place outside the command structure with the establishment of defense agencies and field activities.

division of labor among providers, users, and managers (functional or global combatant commands). These functional or global managers are responsible for integrating common assets supplied by the providers and managing the allocation of these assets to the users of military forces. Although the role of manager has existed for nearly 20 years, it is a role that has thus far been overshadowed by the relationship between providers and users.

In the last several years, revisions to the Unified Command Plan have strengthened the role of global integrators and managers.[9] U.S. Strategic Command has been assigned responsibility for planning and integrating forces for five key mission areas: global strike; intelligence, surveillance, and reconnaissance (ISR); information operations; missile defense; and, most recently, counterproliferation. Similarly, USSOCOM has been given responsibility to plan and integrate operations against terrorist organizations.[10] And, more recently, USJFCOM was assigned responsibility to provide advice to the Secretary of Defense on the peacetime allocation of forces to the regional combatant commands. In each case, the global commands' role as integrator and manager was strengthened with respect to the regional commands, services, and supporting agencies. Providers, managers, and users clearly have been put on a more equal footing. Managers will have a larger say in the allocation of military capabilities, balancing the natural desires of regional commands to want more assets for any given mission and the reluctance of the services to break with normal routines to satisfy combatant commander requests.

---

[9] The Unified Command Plan establishes the missions and geographic responsibilities among the combatant commanders. Among revisions to the plan that took place on October 1, 2002: (1) U.S. Northern Command, a new combatant command, was assigned to defend the United States and support military assistance to civil authorities. Northern Command's headquarters is located at Peterson Air Force Base, Colorado. (2) USJFCOM began to focus on transforming U.S. military forces as geographic responsibilities shifted to Northern and European commands. USJFCOM's headquarters is in Norfolk, Virginia. (3) U.S. Space Command and Strategic Command merged into an expanded Strategic Command, located at Offutt Air Force Base, Nebraska.

[10] Both commands can also be called on to carry out missions assigned by the President and Secretary of Defense.

Whether all inherently joint capabilities should be put under the purview of a global force manager remains an open question. If this were to be the case, the full array of ISR and battle command assets would likely come under joint control. Efforts to place joint combat support assets under the responsibility of U.S. Transportation Command might also increase, perhaps expanding the command's mission to include transportation and materiel support. Moreover, whether or not the role of force managers will expand to give global commands a greater voice in setting requirements to guide the acquisition process also remains an open question.

This new dynamic will have an additional layer of complexity if we are to assume that regional commanders will play less of a role as field commanders and more of a role as strategic advisors and implementers for the President and Secretary of Defense. To the extent this trend continues, the actual users of forces will be the JTF commanders. Regional commanders will, to a growing degree, render advice on the allocation of forces within their areas of responsibility, and USJFCOM will do so for the allocation of forces among regional commanders. The Joint Chiefs of Staff will retain their traditional voice as advisors on the use of service assets in joint contexts. There could be great benefit in these multiple sources of advice. There could also be considerable confusion if the various parties are not privy to the same sources of information.[11]

These changes in the joint division of labor, paired with the observations and recommendations outlined elsewhere in this report, will help create the proper focus and yield the requisite capabilities, including joint tactical interdependencies, that will be necessary to support U.S. strategy and confront the difficult challenges of this era. The next chapter explores the implications of these changes for the military services.

---

[11] On operational matters, for example, it will be essential that the various parties responsible for providing advice are conversant on the JTF commander's plans and recommendations.

CHAPTER FIVE

Implications for the Armed Forces

Realigning the overall division of labor among the armed forces would be but part of the solution needed to align forces and capabilities to support U.S. grand strategy. DoD would also need to field different kinds of forces and capabilities. Here, we explore the implications of our assessment for the overall military establishment.

Building the "Inform and Act" System

Undergirding all the diverse capabilities of the U.S. armed forces are requirements for a new and daunting degree of information—about the enemy, about the environment, and about themselves. These requirements seem likely to grow and diversify. To put the problem in perspective, consider that the U.S. intelligence community had two opportunities to assess Iraq's weapons of mass destruction programs. In 1990, prior to Operation Desert Shield, it substantially underestimated their extent and sophistication. A dozen years later, even after nearly a decade of highly intrusive inspections on the ground in Iraq, it spectacularly overstated the threat. The challenges of identifying the weapons of mass destruction threat in Iraq, along with the so-far unsuccessful manhunts for Osama bin Laden and the Taliban's Mullah Omar, are much more characteristic of the intelligence challenges the nation will face in the future than are the silo- and tank-counting exercises of the Cold War period. Even the most capable joint combat force will have tremendous difficulties succeeding in future complex operations unless it is embedded in an "inform and act" complex that is pervasive and persistent. What this means for DoD is both far reaching and potentially troubling.

We deliberately eschew the terminology of "reconnaissance, surveillance, and target acquisition"; "command, control, communications, computers, intelligence, surveillance, and reconnaissance"; or any other such term for three reasons. First, we want to emphasize the novelty of what will be demanded by a world that is quite different from what the architects of the existing intelligence system envisioned. As the notion of the "battlefield" morphs from clearly delineated geographic areas to specific rooms in particular buildings on the one hand and the attitudes of people of widely varying cultures and backgrounds all around the world on the other; as U.S. forces are called on to grapple with adversaries whose intentions, strengths, and vulnerabilities are radically different from those of its past opponents; and as the United States strives to increase the effectiveness of and reduce dangers to the troops "at the point," the magnitude of the task becomes clear. Second, resorting to the commonplace terminology of the intelligence or command-and-control worlds to describe the challenge would tend to channel thinking about possible solutions into narrow "stovepipes," yet the evidence suggests that an extremely integrated set of capabilities is needed. Finally, the standard terminology tends to drive the discussion to the technical level of platforms, sensors, bandwidth, and the like, while we believe that meeting the challenges of the future is at least as much about people as it is about hardware.

What is called for is an overarching architecture that connects strategic-, operational-, and tactical-level collection, assessment, and dissemination assets and processes with sufficient fidelity and seamlessness to inform decisionmakers at all levels with adequate timeliness and reliability. It is an "effects-based" approach to intelligence, in which the desired effect is the right choice at the right time; it is not "network-centric," it is "decision-centric." A "global information grid" could be a description of one important enabling component, but it is not the architecture itself.

The needed "inform and act" complex will be persistent, profoundly so. How many sensors, including human eyes and ears, will need to stare for how many months at how many patches of mountain or jungle under the attentive control of how many highly trained and experienced analysts to track down the next Osama bin Laden (or even the current one)? What will be needed to locate and target with high confidence every, or at least nearly every, nuclear weapon deployed by a threatening country—and keep them targeted, despite the enemy's sophisticated attempts to conceal and confuse? Just describing the problems briefly suffices to convey their magnitude and difficulty.

Confronting these challenges will not be a task just for DoD; if ever there was a security problem that was truly "interagency," it is this one. Indeed, breaking down institutional and bureaucratic barriers within the newly expanded intelligence community is one of the more formidable aspects of building the complex. Another will be to find the substantial resources that will be needed to devise, develop, and field the systems the complex comprises. Many, such as unmanned aircraft systems (UASs), exist already, but are being procured in inadequate quantities; these problems are easy to fix in theory, however painful the solutions may be programmatically. Other capabilities, such as foliage-penetrating radars or hyperspectral imaging sensors, need infusions of money and ingenuity to reach their military potential, while still other critical pieces are yet to be imagined or, if imagined, remain in an infancy of development. This is clearly an area in which all manner of science and technology investment is needed.

More important than investments in technology, however, will be investments in people. Although computerized algorithms for auto-mated target recognition and similar tasks are potentially very useful adjuncts, the human mind remains our world's most subtle and sophis-ticated analytic tool. It has evolved to see and interpret patterns, to "connect" apparently unrelated "dots," and to create knowledge from what previously were only data. Developing cadres of highly trained personnel to power the "inform and act" architecture, and creating professional trajectories that allow them to employ their skills prof-itably throughout their careers, is a major challenge for the U.S. government—and for the armed forces in particular.

In conjunction with all of this, DoD must continue its efforts to protect its information resources from adversary attack and exploita-tion. As the joint force becomes ever more reliant on timely and massive information flows, likely opponents will almost certainly arrive at the same conclusions that the Chinese apparently already have; namely, that disrupting or distorting U.S. information systems offers a great degree of leverage against the American superpower.[1] It is not only leaders of the U.S. armed forces who dream of convincing the enemy's key weapons that they are "Maytag[s] in a rinse cycle"[2]; similar techniques will be aimed at American forces by adversaries exploiting the diffuse technical sophistication inherent in a globalized world. Cybersecurity will become simultaneously more critical and more complicated as increasing numbers of "non–intelligence community" and non-DoD actors are inevitably engaged in planning, informing, and assessing the nation's security policies and their execution.

Steps that should be considered include the following:

- recruiting and developing a new generation of analysts and intelligence managers with the skills, including language and area training and technical know-how, to deal with the threats emanating from both state and nonstate actors
- realigning development and acquisition priorities to reduce dependence on small numbers of very sophisticated and very expensive platforms and emphasize, instead, more diverse, numerous, and responsive systems (including UASs with the latter characteristics)
- accelerating the operational deployment of advanced sensors that have lingered in the developmental pipeline, as well as developing new classes of networked, inexpensive, "disposable" collection devices, such as air-droppable ground sensors and electro-optical and infrared cameras.

Finally, it will be critical to connect people, platforms, and sensors to one another and to commanders and decisionmakers with hardware, procedures, and processes that are fast, flexible, and robust.

---

[1] For a thorough discussion of China's thinking on information warfare, see Mulvenon and Yang (1999).

[2] General John Jumper, quoted in Tirpak (2004).

A Strategically Decisive Army: Winning at Peace as Well as War

The new American strategy, which now emphasizes expanding the reach of democracy to counter threats from extremism and tyranny, will create extraordinary challenges for the U.S. Army. For the past 50 years, the Army's primary mission has been to win decisively on the conventional battlefield.[3] As discussed in Chapter One, national priorities are now evolving. Motivated by grave threats emanating from illiberal regimes and ill-governed territories, the new grand strategy requires the Army to shoulder a second, coequal, mission: helping to directly and indirectly stabilize key regions.[4]

This strategic evolution poses a dilemma for the Army leadership. On the one hand, it is essential that the Army maintain its hard-earned mastery of conventional warfighting. Decades of extraordinary effort and investment have forged the Army into the world's preeminent instrument of conventional land power, but this preeminence is ephemeral and subject to gradual erosion by innovative adversaries. Sustaining the Army's conventional dominance therefore requires relentless effort and investment in improved conventional capabilities.

On the other hand, the new grand strategy charges the Army with a second mission, stabilization, that is equally demanding and increasingly vital to the nation's security.[5] The new strategy will result in more stability operations that are also more extensive, more complex, more ambitious, and much more important than in past eras.[6] A few of these campaigns may feature direct stability operations, i.e., pacification and counterinsurgency, by Army forces.[7] Most will be less

---

[3] See, for example, J. Wilson (1998).

[4] This is formally enshrined in DoD Directive 3000.05, which states that stability operations are a coequal mission, equivalent in importance to traditional combat operations.

[5] See, for example, U.S. Army Training and Doctrine Command (1999).

[6] Nardulli (2003).

[7] By *direct stability operations*, we are referring to situations in which U.S. forces conduct tactical missions themselves. By *indirect stability operations*, we mean situations in which U.S. forces are acting to expand the capacity of indigenous forces.

direct, consisting mainly of military assistance, advisory, training, and security cooperation missions that indirectly cultivate favorable political conditions in key regions and strengthen the capacity of friendly states to maintain internal security.[8] Still others may involve a mixture of direct and indirect stability operations, as seen today in Iraq and Afghanistan.[9] Whatever the specific context, all are likely to feature a prolonged Army presence, stressful operational and tactical conditions, labyrinthine political-military dynamics, and adaptive adversaries seeking asymmetric advantages. If the Army is to succeed at these complicated and difficult assignments, it will be obliged to devote substantially more effort and resources than heretofore toward organizing, training, and equipping Army forces to conduct stability operations.

Therein lies a dilemma. Sustaining conventional dominance while developing greater proficiency for stability operations may overtax the Army's current institutional capacity. The torque of these twin requirements is straining the Army to the breaking point.[10] Each of these missions is a full-time job. Individual Army units have neither the time nor the institutional support needed to become truly proficient at both missions simultaneously.[11]

Fortunately, the Army Chief of Staff recognizes this dilemma and is moving to better position the Army to fulfill its role in the new grand strategy. Many Army capabilities that are overabundant in the current structure, such as air defense and field artillery, are being downsized to make room for capabilities that are more appropriate to stability operations, such as civil affairs, military police, and special forces.[12]

---

[8]   An example is the Georgia Train and Equip Program (GTEP) conducted by U.S. forces in the Republic of Georgia from 2002 to the present. See U.S. European Command (n.d., ca. 2003).

[9]   Both Operation Enduring Freedom—Afghanistan—and Operation Iraqi Freedom feature direct counterinsurgent operations by U.S. forces complemented by training programs for indigenous forces run by U.S. special forces, allied forces, and conventional U.S. Army units.

[10]   See, for example, DoD (2005a).

[11]   Interviews with Army maneuver unit commanders, March 2005.

[12]   See U.S. Army (2004).

The Army is also reorganizing from a division-based force (33 maneuver brigades in ten divisions) to a modular force of 43 to 48 new-model brigade combat teams that will support a greater presence overseas and that will be individually more balanced and versatile.[13] Personnel and rotational policies are also being revamped to provide more stability for the officer corps and, potentially, more time in assignments to facilitate professional development.[14] These reforms, and many others instituted by the Army Chief of Staff, are broadly commendable and represent an excellent start toward adjusting the service to the new American strategy.

However, fully supporting the strategy will require more work. As impressive as the Army's transformation efforts are, they have yet to address the central dilemma the service faces: how to prepare the Army to excel at conventional warfighting and stability operations simultaneously. For example, while Army doctrine and institutional training continue to focus on conventional warfighting, collective training within many units now focuses exclusively on stability operations.[15] This mismatch degrades proficiency for both missions. Units also continue to be organized and echeloned primarily for the conventional battlefield, then disassembled and reassembled along different lines for deployment to stability operations.[16] Army modernization plans also focus nearly exclusively on conventional mission areas even while the day-to-day focus of the Army acquisition corps is jury-rigging equipment for stability operations.[17] Each of these situations is indicative of the larger challenge the Army faces.

Organizing, Training, and Equipping to Support

To better manage the dilemma the new strategy poses, the Army should consider further reforming its three core Title 10 functions: organizing,

---

[13] Schoomaker and Harvey (2005).

[14] Schoomaker and Harvey (2005).

[15] Interviews with Army and Marine Corps maneuver unit commanders, March 2005.

[16] See Headquarters, Department of the Army (2005).

[17] See Headquarters, Department of the Army (2005).

training, and equipping. The Army might begin by considering adjustments to its long-standing "force package" model of organizing its tactical structure. Under this model, the Army divides its tactical forces
into four packages, each of which is assigned a different role in support of existing operational plans and, in some cases, oriented toward
a particular theater. The force package model allows the Army to tailor
training and equipment for each unit according to its wartime role
while prioritizing modernization and experimentation across the overall force. In the course of QDR implementation, DoD and the Army
will doubtlessly reexamine the existing force packages to account for
the Army's modularity initiative, global posture realignment, and the
aftermath of operations in Iraq. This will present an excellent opportunity to better position the Army to support the new strategy.

In the context of the "1-n-2-1" framework and the stability-versus-
conventional dilemma, the Army should consider realigning its force
packages into one of two mission areas. Specifically, in place of the four
existing force packages, the Army should consider dedicating one force
package to conventional warfighting operations and three force packages to stability operations.

Not unlike the existing arrangement, the new Force Package I
might comprise a small number of dedicated corps and division-level
headquarters, the 15 brigades slated to receive the Future Combat
System (FCS), and the full panoply of active component combat support and combat service support units associated with current and
planned heavy forces.[18] The new Force Package I would be aggressively
modernized and trained to maintain conventional warfighting superiority over potential regional or peer adversaries. As a result, it would
not normally be rotated overseas for stability operations and would not
ordinarily participate in the Army's new three-year force-generation
cycle. Instead, it would focus solely on maintaining peak readiness to
defeat conventional aggression by an emerging peer competitor or to
defeat and depose a regional adversary.

The Army's remaining tactical structure might be grouped into
three force packages, together constituting the Army's contingency

---

[18] Weiner (2005).

forces. They would include light, medium, and heavy maneuver brigades; combat service support echelons; and combat support units relevant to stability operations. The contingency forces would be rotationally available according to the Army's new three-year force-generation cycle (i.e., one force package available at any given time). Their primary mission would be to conduct direct and indirect stability operations, including counterinsurgency, peace operations, military advisory and training missions, and security cooperation activities. They would be "warfighting" units, no less than they are today, but oriented on a different warfighting context. As such, they should incorporate substantial numbers of soldiers with skills in such areas as civil affairs, military police, psychological operations, multinational liaison, and foreign languages, which are not normally found in conventional maneuver brigades. They would also routinely train and operate with Army special forces elements during operations to train, advise, equip, and assist foreign forces.[19] It might even be possible to orient brigades on a particular region of the world to facilitate development of language skills and habitual linkages with special forces groups, service component command headquarters, and combatant command headquarters oriented on the same regions.[20] Organized in this manner, the contingency forces would provide a robust steady-state capacity to conduct both direct and indirect stability operations around the globe.

Despite the prospective benefits of force package realignment, concerns will undoubtedly arise about its long-term ramifications. Some critics may argue that the units in Force Packages II–IV will be nothing more than constabularies, unable to hold their own in serious

---

[19] These units would obviously not be special forces, but they might usefully augment special forces for missions requiring capabilities they already possess, such as training foreign forces. The British Army has used conventional units to train local forces for many years with impressive results.

[20] Some would argue that regional orientation would reduce the flexibility and global deployability of units. However, regional orientation would not preclude deploying units to contingencies in other regions. Moreover, based on experience "cross-leveling" special forces teams outside their assigned regions, there is reason to believe that even units that are oriented on the "wrong" region will likely adjust more quickly than units with no international exposure in the first place. Regional orientation may therefore be a useful step even if the locale of future contingencies cannot be predicted with certainty.

combat. In fact, however, as proposed here, they would be warfighting units possessing the entire suite of combined arms capabilities, merely focused on defeating unconventional and irregular adversaries. Critics might also argue that dividing the Army in this manner will compromise the unity of its professional culture, although the service has used the force package model for many years and has long been divided along branch and specialty lines. Finally, it might be argued that dedicating a portion of the Army's tactical structure to conventional warfighting will exacerbate the existing operational tempo burden on the rest of the force structure. While this may be true, the current "general purpose" approach will, in the context of the new strategy, produce units that are insufficiently proficient in either of the two key mission areas. The Army's first priority must be quality and readiness for the missions required by the new strategy. Whether the Army is large enough to support all the possible operations that might be generated by the new strategy is a separate question.

Stability Operations—Scoping the Demand

We have asserted that the number of regions in which U.S. forces must be prepared to conduct operations against unconventional adversaries is indeterminate. Over the long run, that is correct; but force planners need some sense of demand to inform choices about resource allocation. To that end, we have undertaken a preliminary analysis of potential demand for stability operations over the near- and middle-term planning period, roughly corresponding to the Future Years Defense Plan.

Conceptually, two variables will drive the level of future demand for stability operations. The first is the degree of instability around the world: In how many places might the U.S. government wish to involve itself, over what timeframes, and with what concurrency? The second variable is the manner in which the United States chooses to become involved: How large and direct will its interventions be, and what types of military forces might be involved?

On the first question, our central premise is that it would be imprudent for defense planners to assume that the challenges that insurgents, terrorists, and other irregular threats pose will decline significantly over the relevant planning period. Despite the best efforts, the stability challenge is likely to be at least as serious over the next several years as it is today.

Our data suggest that, of 190-plus states the United Nations recognizes, more than 80 are beset by latent or active instability at the present time.[21] Nearly half involve radical Islamist causes of one sort or another, and more than 12 of these cases linked to Islamism would be considered "actively unstable" by our measures. Of the remaining (i.e., non-Islamist) cases of instability, roughly 15 are actively unstable and the other 30 are latently unstable.

A preliminary measure of aggregate demand for stability operations might therefore posit that, given the new U.S. grand strategy, the U.S. armed forces should be postured to become significantly involved in at least 30 actively unstable states, plus another 20 where latent instability is linked to militant Islamist causes, at any given time. The first category would include countries facing active threats from radical Islamist militants (the Philippines and Afghanistan, for example) and other types of militants as well (Colombia and Nepal, for example). The second category would include such states as Mali and Jordan that face latent threats from Islamist militants. We do not mean to suggest that the United States should or would become involved in every state meeting these criteria. Some states, such as India, will not want or need our assistance in countering insurgent and terrorist groups. Others, such as Indonesia and Uzbekistan, may be all or partly out of bounds

---

[21] To measure contemporary levels of instability, we used data drawn from two publicly available databases maintained by the Jane's Corporation: the "World Insurgency and Terrorism" database and the "Global Insurgency/Terrorism Events" database. The first lists all known active and latent terrorist and insurgent groups. The second records the number of politically motivated incidents of violence that occur in each state every year. We defined any state listed in the first database as sheltering (willingly or otherwise) an active terrorist or insurgent group as an actively unstable country. We also defined any state listed in the second database as averaging more than ten incidents of political violence per year over the past three years as actively unstable. Examples of states that we currently rate as actively unstable include Nepal, Colombia, and the Democratic Republic of the Congo. States listed with latent insurgent and terrorist groups on their soil, or with fewer than ten (but more than zero) incidents of political violence per year over the last three years, were considered latently unstable. Examples include Albania, Niger, and Uganda.

because of human rights or other concerns. Still others may be beyond our help by the time a challenge becomes evident. Yet, in the context of the new grand strategy, a prudent defense posture will provide the capability to support significant commitments to all or most serious cases of instability in a global security context that is neither better nor worse than today's.[22]

This is not to suggest that the U.S. will conduct direct stability operations, on the Iraqi model, in most of these cases. As a rule, U.S. stability operations should (and of necessity, will) be indirect, focused on training, equipping, and advising friendly indigenous forces as they seek to quell their own internal stability challenges. In fact, the U.S. armed forces are already conducting indirect stability operations in many, if not most, of the unstable societies around the world. According to unclassified government reports, the U.S. armed forces deployed mobile training, education, and exercise teams to more than 120 states around the world between 2002 and 2004, averaging more than 350 such deployments per year. But much more could be done were the resources available.[23]

Indirect stability operations are conducted on several levels. At the lowest, most indirect level, small SOF teams visit dozens of friendly nations per year to familiarize partners with U.S. capabilities, gather information, and assist partners in developing their own capabilities in conjunction with DoD security assistance and security cooperation programs.[24]

---

[22] Of course, parametric excursions can help planners better understand the dimensions of the challenge. If planners were to assume that the stability challenge will grow by 20 percent, for example, this would yield an aggregate demand of approximately 36 actively unstable states and 25 latently unstable states with Islamist challenges. Alternatively, if planners were to assume that the stability challenge would ease by 20 percent over the planning timeframe, this would yield an aggregate demand of 24 actively unstable states and 15 latently unstable states with Islamist challenges.

[23] DoD and Department of State (2002–2004).

[24] In fact the lines are fuzzy between small-scale indirect stability operations, security assistance programs, and security cooperation activities. From the strategic perspective, they are indistinguishable.

At a higher level, sustained and sizable U.S. train, equip, and advise operations are conducted in such places as Colombia, the Philippines, and the Republic of Georgia. In these indirect stability operations, the United States provides a suite of capabilities to partner armed forces to enable them to deal with internal security threats.

At a still larger level, major train, equip, and advise operations are combined with limited U.S. direct stability operations in such places as Afghanistan and the Horn of Africa. In these instances, limited U.S. and Western forces undertake a limited range of missions against key adversaries in the region, while the primary effort of the operation remains training, equipping, and advising local forces to create indigenous capabilities to cope with threats to stability.

The direct stability operations of the sort conducted in Iraq are the largest and costliest variant of stability operations, exceptional for their very scope and complexity. In these cases, U.S. forces have assumed primary responsibility for stability in another state. The resulting demands are enormous.

Our assessment of the threats posed by terrorist and insurgent groups and of the capacity of U.S. armed forces to address these threats suggests that the U.S. armed forces should be postured to conduct stability operations in approximately 50 states around the world at any given time. These operations will include a mix of small indirect stability operations and large direct stability operations, heavily weighted toward the former. The nature of the operations is such that most of these demands will fall on the Army and Marine Corps, as well as the special forces. We therefore believe the Army should be structured to conduct both large direct stability operations (as the exception) and multiple, concurrent, moderately sized, and prolonged indirect stability operations around the world as a matter of course.[25]

Training

In addition to structuring itself to better support the new grand strategy, the Army should consider altering aspects of its recruiting, train-

---

[25] We believe the Marine Corps should also adjust its approach to such operations, as detailed below.

ing, and education system. Most importantly, the basic intellectual framework for the Army—its field manuals (FMs); tactics, techniques, and procedures (TTP) handbooks; and combined arms training strategy plans—should be reoriented to mirror the coequal status of conventional warfighting and stability operations under the new grand strategy. At the lower tactical levels, the Army might find it advantageous to maintain two parallel sets of doctrine and training products, one for units in Force Package I and another for contingency units in Force Packages II through IV.[26] The Army has more than a decade of experience maintaining parallel doctrine and training materials for "digitized" and "nondigitized" forces that can serve as a model in this regard.[27]

Similarly, the Army should consider reorienting the curricula at the service's professional military education institutions to establish a new balance between warfighting and stability operations. The content of most curricula need not be changed because they possess equal relevance for both mission areas (e.g., the military decisionmaking process and combined arms tactics). Course content applicable solely to conventional warfighting (e.g., deep attack) would in general be replaced by stability operations content, as this will be most relevant to the sizable majority of officers who will be going to contingency force units in their next assignment. To ensure that officers in conventional warfighting units maintain peak proficiency, a dedicated schoolhouse might be collocated with the Force Package I corps headquarters to provide extra

---

[26] For example, the Army might consider rebalancing capstone Army doctrine (i.e., FM 3-0, Operations) and operational-level doctrine to give equal weight to warfighting and stability operations. Tactical doctrine, TTPs, and training literature might best be issued in two forms, one focused on conventional warfighting and another focused on stability operations. Units in III Corps would train to the warfighting doctrine; contingency force units would train to the stability doctrine.

[27] III Corps headquarters, the 4th Infantry Division (Mechanized), and the 1st Cavalry Division are the Army's first digitized units. A parallel set of field manuals, TTPs, and training products have been developed to enable these units to exploit their new digital battle command system.

exposure to these issues. Again, the digitization experience provides a model.[28]

Over time, these changes to the Army's education and training structure, coupled with new patterns of deployment and operations, will significantly alter the skill mix of the officer corps. The Army would become broadly more proficient in stability operations and broadly less practiced at conventional warfighting. However, units specializing in conventional warfighting could actually be expected to be more proficient than today's units, which attempt to train for both warfighting and stability operations. Units specializing in stability operations would likely be much more proficient than today's forces. The result would be an Army better postured and prepared to support the new grand strategy.

Equipping the Force

Finally, the Army should also consider certain adjustments to its materiel investment plans. The FCS program is currently the centerpiece of these plans.[29] The FCS program is intended to produce a new family of armored vehicles that will be linked together at every echelon by an advanced digital information system. Generally speaking, the primary objective of the FCS program is to enable the Army to sustain its tactical superiority over conventional opponents indefinitely. This objective, in and of itself, is laudable.

However, within its modernization program, the Army should consider reallocating research, development, and procurement resources toward enhancing the capabilities of individual soldiers. Current Army modernization plans focus heavily on new platforms and their associated systems. Relatively little is devoted to what are termed "soldier systems."[30] For more than a decade, the Army has had a program on the books called "Land Warrior" that aims to provide an integrated suite of miniaturized digital communications, improved ballistic pro-

---

[28] The Fort Hood Battle Command Training Center, which trains officers transitioning to III Corps units on digitized doctrine and TTP, provides a model in this regard.

[29] U.S. Army (2005, pp. 10–11).

[30] For a summary of soldier modernization priorities, see U.S. Army (2005, pp. 13–14).

tection, advanced night vision, more-lethal individual weapons, and other improved kit to individual soldiers. Over the years, the Army has consistently placed a lower priority on Land Warrior than on platform-based systems, resulting in many delays and setbacks. Given the new operational environment and the demands of the new grand strategy, the Army should consider significantly expanding the resources it devotes to soldier modernization in general and to Land Warrior more specifically.

A New Air-Ground Partnership

The new strategy will likely call on air and land forces to partner in new ways. In some cases, U.S. air forces will partner with local ground forces to help an emerging democracy defeat internal threats, such as insurgency and terrorism. In other cases, coalition air forces will partner with special forces and indigenous ground forces to conduct counterterrorist missions. Finally, in major combat operations, air and land forces will increasingly combine in modular, responsive, and agile packages to protect friendly nations from external aggression or to take down regimes.

Recent operations in Afghanistan and Iraq illustrate how effective these innovative partnerships can be. In Afghanistan, coalition special forces directed precision air strikes against enemy forces. Special forces, sometimes working alone but usually integrated with friendly indigenous ground forces, were able to detect and identify targets impossible to identify from the air alone. U.S. Air Force terminal attack controllers working on the ground with U.S. Army and coalition special forces directed air strikes that were precise and at times massive. Air and ground forces working together presented the Taliban with a dilemma: If they dispersed to avoid air attack, they would be overrun by anti-Taliban forces; if they concentrated to defend against ground attack, they became vulnerable to devastating air attack. They generally chose the latter and suffered greatly as a result. In short, air strikes tipped the balance of power in favor of the Northern Alliance and other friendly

Afghan forces, allowing them to break a stalemate that had lasted for years, defeat Taliban forces, and overthrow the government.[31]

U.S. ground maneuver forces subsequently deployed into the country to conduct counterterrorism and stability operations. These ground forces deployed to Afghanistan without their artillery, counting on rotary- and fixed-wing aircraft to provide needed fire support. In operations since the fall of the Taliban, air forces have played a vital supporting role in Afghanistan, providing essential lift, intelligence, and strike support. Coalition air forces have prevented insurgents from massing and provided on-call fire support for Afghan and U.S. forces. This has allowed small units of coalition forces to patrol effectively, without the risk of being overwhelmed by superior numbers.

In Operation Iraqi Freedom, air-ground synergies were again exploited in what were largely simultaneous air-ground offensives. To speed the movement of ground forces into the Gulf and make them more agile on the battlefield, the Army deployed about half the fire support capacity that it took with it to Operation Desert Storm in 1991.[32] Relying heavily on air forces for close support and being less encumbered by the need to move large artillery formations and tons of ammunition, the Army drove rapidly up the west side of the Euphrates River valley. The Marines, who had decided to supplement relatively limited artillery support with air power decades earlier, made similar progress to the east in the drive on Baghdad.

Coalition air attacks sapped the morale of soldiers in the Iraqi Army and Republican Guard, interdicted Iraqi forces that sought to move, destroyed many in defensive positions or hides, and protected flanks. Although far from perfect, the combination of airborne ISR and strike gave Army commanders sufficient confidence that they allowed lead elements, such as the 3/7 Cavalry, to operate well ahead of other friendly forces. Without such air dominance, these forces would have risked being cut off and destroyed by counterattacking Iraqi forces.

---

[31] For a more-detailed discussion of how air and ground forces worked together in Operation Enduring Freedom, see Pirnie et al. (2005).

[32] As measured by the fire support potential (in tons) per maneuver brigade. See Pirnie et al. (2005, p. 134).

Although the Iraqis were able to move several brigades a few hundred miles into new defensive positions without being detected and attacked by air, they were in no case able to conduct operationally significant counteroffensives.[33] Finally, U.S. Navy, Marine, and Air Force aircraft became the first choice for close support for most ground forces, especially in built-up areas where the risk of collateral damage limited the use of artillery.

The new strategy will look to air-ground forces to protect emerging democracies from external threats and, in the extreme, take down regimes that are a threat to their neighbors or that threaten the international order more broadly. During the Cold War, the United States was able to focus its planning and posture for large-scale combat on two primary areas and to forward deploy substantial combat power accordingly. Today, the threat is less focused, and U.S. air and ground forces could be called to project power in many regions of the globe. This has led both the Army and the Air Force to emphasize expeditionary capabilities.

As the Army moves toward lighter and more-agile forces, it increasingly views air power as indispensable, both for ISR and for on-call fires. Airmen are generally enthusiastic about these new opportunities to partner with the Army but have some reservations about the high costs of providing on-call airpower 24 hours a day, for weeks or months on end over a large battlespace. If this were to become the dominant preoccupation of U.S. air forces, it might require a very large force structure and render airpower a passive instrument waiting to be called into action. Airmen argue that on-call fires should be limited in time and space—for example, provided during a major offensive but not during routine operations. Air operations instead would be used primarily to create opportunities for ground force maneuver, to protect exposed flanks, and to interdict enemy forces far beyond friendly forces. At the same time, ground maneuver should be used to make enemy forces more vulnerable to detection and attack from the air. In a true partnership, air and ground forces would be viewed as mutually

---

[33] See U.S. Army (2003), especially Chapters 4 and 5.

enabling, shifting back and forth between supported and supporting roles.

Major combat operations like these will remain important, but, as we observed in Chapter Two, potential enemies recognize the risks and costs associated with fighting the United States and its allies head-on and are adapting their strategies and capabilities accordingly. Hence, such large-scale combat may be the exception rather than the rule. More commonly, the military role in defending U.S. interests will be less direct. Often, forward-deployed forces will be central to assuring regional stability within which regimes can liberalize successfully, and this function must be factored into forward-basing decisions. In many cases, the primary security problem emerging democracies face will be internal. In these cases, the greatest contribution that U.S. forces can make is in training, equipping, and advising host-nation forces. In some circumstances, U.S. forces may go beyond security assistance and provide operational support to local forces in the form of lift, ISR, or fire support.

Defeating an insurgency requires the local government to convince the populace that it can provide security and govern effectively. Although foreign troops (e.g., U.S.) may improve the security situation in the short run, dependence on them undermines the credibility and legitimacy of the local government. Nationalist sentiments can be easily manipulated against the "occupiers," fueling an insurgency that otherwise could have been defeated with local forces alone.[34] Thus, U.S. forces need to keep a low profile in counterinsurgency operations.

One interesting option worth pursuing is the partnering of U.S. air assets (which can often keep a low profile) with local ground forces. Local ground forces have many potential advantages: They know the local environment, customs, and language and can (at least in theory) gather intelligence more easily from the civilian population; they are acclimatized to the weather and terrain; and their casualties are not carried daily in U.S. papers. If professionally led, their presence enhances rather than undermines confidence in the national government. With the right training and equipment, which may often come from U.S.

---

[34] For a thoughtful analysis of this problem, see Metz and Millen (2004).

ground forces, they can be highly effective. U.S. air forces can provide powerful force multipliers, such as enduring airborne surveillance of key areas, surge lift capacity for major operations, and precision strike. Over time, the United States will want to help friendly nations develop an indigenous ability to conduct these missions, but in the short run, U.S. air forces may need to provide these capabilities.

Integrating Air, Space, and Maritime Power

The new grand strategy offers three broad roles for air, space, and maritime forces, within each of which lie a number of challenging responsibilities: protecting the commons, projecting power against state adversaries, and defeating terrorist groups abroad.

Protecting the Commons

Freedom of innocent navigation through the air, on the high seas, and in near-earth space is a critical component of any peaceful and prosperous global order. While the dictates of international law and the actions of supranational bodies can be counted on to govern the actions of respectable parties, the ability to enforce these norms is needed as both a deterrent to misbehavior and, on occasion, to punish noncompliance. As the dominant military power in all three media, the United States should expect to be a major contributor to efforts in these directions and, as the services charged with maintaining the nation's main capabilities in the air, at sea, and in outer space, the Air Force and Navy will carry the main responsibility for the nation.

There may be nothing particularly new in this assignment. What may be changing, however, is the nature and extent of possible challenges to the generally peaceful global regime. While nonbelligerent air and maritime traffic has often been at risk in the context of conflicts among nations—the Iran-Iraq war being one recent example—the threat from subnational terrorist and guerrilla organizations appears to be increasing, as witnessed by the SAM engagements of an Israeli airliner in Kenya in 2002, a DHL cargo jet in Baghdad in 2003, and al Qaeda's attack on a French oil tanker off Yemen in 2002. And the historical sanctuary of space may also be eroding as technologies enabling destruction, disablement, or interference with satellite functions become more widely available to states and subnational groups. The image of 21st-century "Barbary pirates" exploiting modern technology to interfere with peaceful and necessary uses of air, sea, and space may be a little exaggerated but nonetheless looms as a possibility.[35]

Dealing with possible threats to this global commons requires, above all, enhanced situational awareness and responsiveness in all three media, especially in space and at sea. The Air Force is currently pursuing several initiatives, including the Rapid Attack Identification Detection and Reporting System and the Space-Based Space Surveillance System, intended to improve its ability to sense and assess attacks on space assets. Whether or not these specific programs are the right or complete solutions, their purpose is an important one. The Air Force should also continue efforts to develop capabilities to rapidly deploy affordable replacement or supplementary satellites so that crucial space-based functions are not lost or impaired. Both military and civilian space planners have worked to achieve this long-sought capability for a number of years, but the cost per pound of payload orbited and the overall pace of launch preparation and on-orbit checkout have not improved dramatically. New energy (and resources) may need to be injected, and, as businesses and individuals around the world become more dependent on such widely available space-based "utilities" as communications and navigation, military efforts may need to expand to encompass protecting and augmenting civilian and international space capabilities.

An alternative approach to ensuring the availability of critical capabilities could be to place the appropriate payloads on platforms that operate within the atmosphere rather than on satellites. High-altitude, long-endurance aircraft—presumably unmanned—can act as sensor platforms, communication relays, and even GPS transmitters.

---

[35] These "pirates" can (and do) also attack activities in a fourth critical medium, cyberspace. While DoD has a substantial job to do in ensuring that its own cyber infrastructure is secure from disruption and exploitation—as we discuss briefly below—it plays little or no role in protecting the civilian commons in this area.

Lighter-than-air vehicles operating above 65,000 feet, a domain often referred to as "near-space," might perform the same functions. Pending breakthroughs in space launch capabilities, it may prove far less expensive to provide hedges against the loss of key satellites in this way.

At sea, the U.S. Navy has begun adapting to the new security environment. The February 2006 draft U.S. Navy strategy, *Navy's 3/1 Strategy*, devotes most of its attention to U.S. Navy's role in the global war on terrorism, stability operations, and homeland defense and security.[36] U.S. Navy's challenge in these areas is primarily to increase its wide-area surveillance capabilities. A naval task group's field of view is fairly large, but the oceans are far larger. Combating piracy and other threats to freedom of navigation arising outside of classic state-to-state warfare is likely to demand a surveillance "footprint" that is larger than what traditional naval assets can maintain, that can penetrate areas inhospitable to these assets, and that is both more persistent and more distributed geographically than these forces can sustain. Land-based manned aircraft, such as the venerable P-3, remain valuable for these missions. U.S. Navy plans to replace the P-3 with the P-8 Multimission Maritime Aircraft (a military variant of the successful Boeing 737 commercial jet) will give U.S. Navy a platform with greater range, endurance, and payload. U.S. Navy should also be encouraged to continue its efforts to develop and field the Broad Area Maritime Surveillance UAS, a version of the Air Force's Global Hawk that both has a longer on-station time than any manned aircraft and is less reliant on relatively nearby land basing. Finally, U.S. Navy efforts to develop surface combatants optimized for littoral warfare are also important. The first Littoral Combat Ship, the USS *Freedom*, will reach the fleet in 2007. "Designed to counter challenging shallow-water threats in coastal regions, specifically mines, diesel submarines and fast surface craft," these ships will significantly enhance U.S. Navy capabilities to deal with opponents ranging from pirates to more-conventional adversaries.[37]

---

[36] U.S. Department of the Navy (2006).

[37] "Navy to Base First Littoral Combat Ship in San Diego" (2005).

Projecting Power

We argued in the previous section that the Army has a predominant role to play in crucial and difficult counterterrorism, advisory, and nation assistance operations. We argue below that the Marine Corps is uniquely suited to a new and deeply synergistic relationship with the joint special operations community. While air and naval forces will make important contributions in these areas, the core future challenge they confront is projecting U.S. power against state adversaries. As we discussed in Chapter Two, these campaigns are markedly less likely than in the past to be centered on large armies committing aggression across land borders. Instead, the threats of primary concern will arise from small- to medium-sized arsenals of nuclear weapons (and other so-called "weapons of mass destruction"), larger numbers of conventionally armed ballistic and cruise missiles, and other modern "anti-access" capabilities.[38] Defeating enemies thus armed seems to call for the kinds of responsive and flexible surveillance and fire capabilities that U.S. air and maritime forces field, and the requirements of such conflicts should to a large extent guide both Air Force and U.S. Navy modernization programs.

Both as delivery systems for nuclear weapons and as "conventional" threats to U.S. and allied bases and other infrastructure targets, ballistic and cruise missiles demand a robust and effective set of counters. The U.S. Navy is set to field a wide-area defense system against TBMs, based on the Aegis radar and an upgraded variant of Standard Missile. Early tests of this system have been promising, although some hurdles are still to be overcome. If effective, the SM-3 will be capable of intercepting TBMs outside the atmosphere.[39] Land-based terminal-phase interceptors, such as the Patriot missile, are unlikely to defend

---

[38] These include emerging threats to maritime forces, including those presented by quiet submarines, advanced torpedoes and mines, and antiship cruise missiles. Modern long-range air defenses, including radar-guided SAMs and fourth-generation fighters with beyond-visual-range missiles, can also threaten air forces' access to bases and to important operating areas. And weapons that can interfere with or disable satellites, including ground-based lasers, jammers, and co-orbital kinetic kill vehicles, can threaten satellites that provide essential capabilities to U.S. expeditionary operations.

[39] U.S. Department of the Navy (2004, pp. 72–73).

air bases and other key facilities effectively unless combined with mid-course interceptors, such as the SM-3, so this capability will be in great demand to defend targets ashore. While missile-defense capabilities are a potentially significant contribution to success in future wars, demand for these systems may constrain the ability of the United States to employ its surface naval power in other, more-traditional, sea-control and power-projection tasks. Concerns over losing operational flexibility may in part explain why the U.S. Navy plans in the near term to procure only a small number of interceptor missiles. Both the potential of the system and the yawning gap between needed and fielded defensive capabilities suggest that it should expand and accelerate production and fielding of this system, assuming that it continues to do well in testing. Indeed, the size of the Aegis-equipped destroyer and cruiser fleet or the "buy" of midcourse missile-defense interceptors may need to take into account a ballistic missile-defense role that goes beyond protecting the fleet.

The Air Force's future in missile defense lies in two principal areas. It will maintain its traditional role of providing missile warning and attack assessment with the much-delayed and overrun-plagued Space-Based Infrared System satellites. A second, and new, mission area is boost-phase defense, for which the AL-1A Airborne Laser aircraft is the only system currently in advanced development. It has suffered several technical problems and, in any case, may never be procured in large numbers. Even if it is fielded, its capabilities may prove to be limited against the most important and dangerous threats, which likely will be beyond its effective range in many scenarios. If defending against ballistic missiles is *the* game, The Air Force will need to pursue concepts and capabilities beyond the Space-Based Infrared and the Airborne Laser systems if it wants make an important contribution.

Countering TBMs and cruise missiles has, of course, an offensive component as well. And neutralizing an adversary's nuclear and anti-access arsenals will likewise involve going after an array of difficult targets on an enemy's territory. These include small mobile targets, such as missile transporter-erector-launchers, and hardened, deeply buried targets, such as nuclear weapon storage sites. Currently, deployed forces do not have impressive capabilities against either type of target.

Depending on the terrain and the enemy's concept of operations, just discovering either a mobile transporter-erector-launcher or the precise location of an underground facility can be exceedingly difficult.

While this is not just an Air Force problem, the Air Force will obviously play a major role in any intelligence architecture that manages to make significant inroads on the problem of mobile and hidden targets. Space radar and the E-10 aircraft are potentially important contributors, but both face development and acquisition challenges and would not represent a total solution in any event.[40] Promising approaches that merit further examination include fielding a high-endurance, stealthy UAS that can loiter in enemy airspace; acquiring new-generation sensors, such as hyperspectral imaging systems, that can penetrate many types of camouflage and cover; and developing new munitions, perhaps including high-speed standoff weapons that can substantially shorten the time between detecting a mobile target and successfully engaging it.

Hardened and deeply buried targets likewise present serious challenges. Ultimately, the diggers of tunnels will always be able to go deeper than the weapons we might devise to get at them can, so the United States is at some level destined to lose this contest. But DoD must keep working on concepts to bottle up, if not to destroy, assets that enemies might try to bury. As with mobile targets, gaining good information about the location, construction, and layout of such facilities is the sine qua non of attacking them effectively. This requirement creates tremendous demands for day-to-day surveillance of activities in countries with which our forces might go to war. Specialized weapons to close portals, destroy support systems (such as ventilation ducts), and to deny personnel access to buried facilities are also called for.

Another response to growing threats from ballistic and cruise missiles is to procure and field air forces that are less dependent on access to bases within range of the most numerous of these systems.[41] The

---

[40] Indeed, the decision was taken in the 2005 QDR to eliminate the procurement phase of the E-10 program.

[41] In a sense, this is a "new" old problem. Soviet and Warsaw Pact forces threatened NATO air bases throughout the Cold War. However, in the past 15 years, U.S. air forces have been

Air Force's current and programmed force structures rely heavily on mostly single-seat fighters with a relatively short unrefueled range for sustained combat operations. While these aircraft have proven themselves capable of undertaking missions over long ranges, they require extensive support from air-to-air refueling tankers (which themselves must be based somewhere in the vicinity). These aircraft also have a limited payload-carrying capability, which, coupled with low sortie rates due to long mission durations, translates into fewer kills per aircraft per day.

The desirability of longer-range systems is likely to increase for three reasons. First, the threat to land bases from nuclear weapons; conventional missiles; and unconventional forces, such as SOF and terrorists, is increasing. Second—in part but only in part—because of this, the issues associated with political access are unlikely to get easier. Air Force operations since 1973 and through Operation Iraq Freedom have frequently been impeded by the inability to gain needed basing and overflight rights from even close allies, and—as exemplified in recent comments by President Roh Moo-Hyun of South Korea—these challenges remain.[42] Third, in some important scenarios—a China-Taiwan showdown being the clearest example—there is simply a dearth of attractive options for basing short-range combat aircraft. A more-robust mix of longer- and shorter-range platforms, which could include combat UASs, would offer joint commanders important flexibility in solving their most pressing operational and tactical problems.[43]

An advantage of navies for power projection is their relative independence from land bases. Modern surface ships and submarines can operate for weeks at a time, ranging over thousands of miles, with-

---

able to operate from land bases with relative impunity. We believe the relative luxury of these circumstances is coming rapidly to an end.

[42] In remarks at the South Korean Air Force Academy, Roh stated that U.S. forces based in Korea would not be used for operations off the peninsula without the permission of the Seoul government. See Shim (2005). For an extended discussion of the political calculus of access, see Shlapak, Stillion, et al. (2002).

[43] As a complement to a realigned force mix, the Air Force should also consider investing in greater capabilities to fight effectively out of bases that are under attack, which it worked extensively when it faced the Warsaw Pact in Europe.

out resupply from port, a quality prized in theaters where access to land bases may be questionable because of uncertainty about coalition politics or growing threats to fixed facilities. In antiaccess scenarios in which the operations of U.S. surface combatants may initially be constrained, submarines are likely to make significant contributions by rolling back adversary attack submarines, launching cruise missiles against high-value land targets, inserting SOF, planting mines, and attacking enemy surface combatants. Surface combatants, in addition to their significant firepower and antisubmarine warfare capabilities, may be uniquely positioned to jam enemy satellite communications; they might also play a significant role in other information operations. Offsetting these strengths to some extent are limitations the Navy faces in mounting sustained, large-scale offensive operations ashore, especially over longer distances. Even a *Nimitz*-class aircraft carrier can launch and recover only around 100 to 150 sorties per day on a sustained basis—the equivalent of about 30 B-52 sorties—and at all but the shortest ranges, their fighters must rely on land-based tankers for support. Carrier-based aircraft also face payload limits, and, until the fielding of the F-35, all lack stealth, which will be crucial to maintaining reasonable survivability against modern air defense weapons, such as the Russian-built SA-10 and SA-20.[44]

In the end, the United States will be able to succeed in the most-demanding power-projection tasks of the future only if the land- and sea-based components operate together, capitalizing on each other's respective strengths and compensating for areas of relative weakness. This means that when basing for land-based fighters is in short supply, sea-based forces should be prepared to take the lead in carrying the fight ashore, with the important assistance of Air Force tankers, bombers, and surveillance assets based more remotely. Similarly, when fixed-wing naval aircraft are of limited use—perhaps because the air defense environment is at least initially too severe or the distances to the targets are too great—the joint commander can still exploit sea-based theater

---

[44] Sea-launched Tomahawk cruise missiles are a valuable strike asset that can be employed in the presence of moderately advanced threats, and the Navy plans to continue evolving the system to make it more flexible.

missile defense to protect air bases ashore and land-attack missile forces to enable and amplify Air Force use of its stealthier, more-survivable fleet to greatest effect. Another possibility would seek to defeat mobile targets (antiship missiles, SAMs, TBMs) operating in coastal areas by teaming Air Force surveillance assets with standoff weapons launched from submarines. If these targets could be detected and tracked for a few tens of minutes, they would be vulnerable to attack by subsonic land-attack cruise missiles launched from nuclear attack or guided-missile submarines.[45] Efforts should be made to formalize, facilitate, and expand cooperation between the Navy and Air Force so that effective joint operations can be mounted even when significant portions of each service's force "package" are, for one reason or another, not available.

Defeating Terrorist and Insurgent Groups Abroad

While the main focus of Air Force and Navy should be on dealing with the dangerous challenges state adversaries present, both services also have important roles to play in neutralizing terrorist and insurgent groups threatening the United States or its friends and allies. Both services will be called on to provide surveillance assets; one initiative worth pursuing might be the development of a UAS that is smaller and less costly than the Predator class, but substantially more capable in terms of range, endurance, and payload than the "tactical" UASs the Army and Marines are fielding. Properly trained personnel, with appropriate area experience and language skills, will be needed to make sense of the intelligence "take," as well as to interact with host countries as trainers and advisors.

For the Air Force, training and advising friendly governments will require frequent, small, prolonged, and widespread deployments, cre-

---

[45] We have in mind here targets operating in an area within roughly 100 miles of the coast. The relationship between U.S. tracking capabilities and the weapon's time of flight is key. If the United States can detect but only briefly track targets, delivery must be extremely rapid, which would likely lead to a need for very-long-endurance loitering or hypersonic solutions. If, however, tracking for low double-digit minutes is possible, less-exotic weapons—such as the cruise missile described above, enhanced perhaps by the limited loiter time that the new Tactical Tomahawk now coming into the inventory offers—become feasible.

ating additional demands for force-protection concepts and resources. Capabilities needed for direct support of both U.S. and non-U.S. forces engaged in combat operations will include surveillance; mobility; combat search-and-rescue; medical evacuation; and, from time to time, fire support. For the last role, some variety of "gunship-like" platform could prove very valuable.[46]

The Navy's SEALs, like all other elements of America's SOF, are already deeply engaged in the war on terror. Like the other services, the Navy should be directed to develop cadres of sailors who, while not trained to the same level and range of skills as special forces, have the language and cultural background and the technical skills needed to be highly effective as trainers and advisors to friendly governments and militaries. Naval warships and surveillance aircraft will also be employed in helping monitor and intercept questionable maritime traffic in important areas around the world.

Of particular importance will be a long-term effort to develop the sorts of officers and noncommissioned officers needed for conducting sustained noncombat operations in foreign countries. Both services should take the initiative to create and fund a true foreign area officer program and career path, along the lines of the Army's program of the same name.

Getting More from the Corps

Dating back to the development of the Advance Base concept and large-scale amphibious warfare between the world wars, the Marines have a demonstrated history of understanding national priorities and reforming themselves to match these priorities. The present is no exception. The Marine Corps has adopted a number of innovations dating back to before 9/11, including, for example, forming a Chemical-Biological Response Force and an Antiterrorism Brigade to better serve

---

[46] By *gunship-like*, we mean a weapon system that combines fairly long range, a reasonable degree of survivability against low to medium threats, a deep and flexible magazine of ordnance, long endurance, and adequate communications and sensor capabilities to fight safely and effectively in conjunction with hotly engaged friendly ground forces.

the new grand strategy. The question is whether even more should be done. One opportunity seems especially promising: integrating the Marines more completely with the nation's SOF.

The Marine Corps already has a long history of robust cooperation with SOF. When USSOCOM was originally formed in 1987, the Marine Corps held its distance and did not form a service special operations component as the other services did. Elite Marine units, such as force reconnaissance companies, were not placed under USSOCOM's control in the same way that Army Special Forces, SEALs, Air Force Special Forces, and Rangers were provided by their respective services. However, the Marine Corps did create a program to train Marine expeditionary units (MEUs) to support and conduct a number of SOF-type missions, such as direct action and special reconnaissance.[47] MEUs with this training were certified as "special operations–capable" but retained their traditional mission of conducting six-month deployments around the world as an emergency response force and lever of diplomatic influence. Special operations–capable MEUs routinely incorporated SOF elements before 9/11. Since 9/11, the Marine-SOF relationship has grown even closer. Marine officers have commanded large SOF elements in recent operations, such as Operation Enduring Freedom—Afghanistan—and JTF Horn of Africa, and a Marine officer served for a time as the USSOCOM chief of staff. The Marines have resurrected their force reconnaissance elements and air-naval gunfire liaison companies to support, *inter alia*, SOF operations.

However, there may be yet more opportunities to expand Marine-SOF integration in support of the new grand strategy. One key Marine Corps role has traditionally been to provide a steady-state presence of three MEUs afloat in the Mediterranean, western Pacific, and Arabian Gulf at any given time. MEUs are natural partners for SOF units. The battalion of Marines at the heart of the MEU is well suited to serve

---

[47] An MEU is a task force built around a ground combat element (a reinforced infantry battalion), an aviation combat element (a composite squadron of CH-53E, AH-1W, UH-1N, and AV-8B aircraft), a combat service support element (a MEU service support group), and a command element (joint command and control and all-source ISR). An amphibious ready group normally consists of three Navy ships, an amphibious assault ship, an amphibious transport dock, and a dock landing ship. See Headquarters U.S. Marine Corps (2001).

as a quick-reaction force to support small SOF teams in trouble; the MEU's aircraft provide a useful degree of mobility and firepower to SOF units; and the MEU's ships provide off-shore basing (for SOF aircraft and watercraft) and a safe sanctuary *in extremis*. Furthermore, the MEU's officers and noncommissioned officers are world-class trainers and could potentially complement the overstretched reservoir of SOF advisory assistance teams.[48] The promise of the MEU-SOF partnership is therefore easy to see.

At present, however, the benefits of the MEU-SOF partnership cannot be fully realized because MEU deployments and SOF operations are not as closely coordinated as they might be. Generally speaking, the patrol locations for each MEU are selected well in advance of the group's departure. Furthermore, this presence is not typically coordinated to coincide with SOF presence on the ground. As a result, MEUs are often poorly positioned to support contingency SOF missions, and SOF planners cannot rely on the presence of a MEU, which obliges them to develop plans and training scenarios under the assumption that a MEU will not be available to support a given mission. To remedy this situation, DoD should consider taking three steps:

1. Consider expanding MEU coverage in the world or, alternately, invest in the capability to surge MEUs or MEU-like assets to support contingency operations.
2. Expeditiously implement proposals for a Joint Presence Policy so that, among other needs, Marine Corps and SOF deployments can be more tightly coupled.
3. Incorporate MEU assets routinely in SOF exercises.

Additionally, the MEU ships already provide excellent platforms for surveillance and reconnaissance. Beyond the MEU's own assets, it is conceivable that sensors might be developed for aircraft, perhaps UASs, capable of operating from the LHD-class ships in amphibi-

---

[48] In fact, the Marine Corps may soon adopt such a supporting role for special forces training missions in Africa, see Ma (2005).

ous readiness groups.[49] LHDs resemble small aircraft carriers. Initial research indicates that LHDs could support flight operations by large conventional UASs, such as Global Hawk and Predator, only after major modifications to the ships (catapults, arresting wires, barriers, etc.) and the UASs themselves (arresting gear, strengthened undercarriage, etc.). However, vertical-takeoff-and-landing UASs, such as the HV-911 Eagle Eye tilt-rotor UAS being procured by the Coast Guard and the helicopter-like RQ-8 Fire Scout UAS being procured by the Navy, might be natural candidates for reconnaissance and surveillance operations off LHD-class vessels. This might provide another flexible, persistent, and difficult-to-counter reconnaissance and surveillance option to support operations in key regions.

Security Cooperation in the New Security Environment

The new security environment calls for a security cooperation effort greatly expanded over that of the past 15 years. Security cooperation can help establish the preconditions for a successful transition to democratic rule by inculcating democratic values among commissioned and noncommissioned officers in the host-nation military. It also is essential to help emerging democracies deter and defeat external and internal threats.

Security cooperation has been an important part of U.S. foreign and defense policy for nearly a century.[50] The United States has used it to provide material support to allies during wars, to support diplomacy, and to help friendly nations improve their ability to defend against

---

[49] The LHA and LHD classes both have large flight decks that run the length of the ship, along with substantial hangar space below decks. They also have a large well deck and other facilities to support amphibious operations.

[50] Security cooperation (formerly security assistance) consists of several programs authorized by the U.S. Foreign Assistance Act of 1961 (and amendments), the Arms Export Control Act (and amendments), and related statutes. Foreign military sales and international military education and training are the two major programs. See Defense Security Cooperation Agency (2005). In addition, the combatant commanders and military services interact routinely with foreign military forces as part of DoD security cooperation activities.

internal and external foes. The United States provides military aid to nations in every region of the globe, funding roughly $4.6 billion in foreign military financing and $91 million in international military education and training in FY 2004. Yet 90 percent of the foreign military financing funds go to just six nations, leaving roughly $500 million for the rest of the world.[51] Although these programs have been effective in achieving U.S. objectives in the past, they may need to adapt to new circumstances and goals. To defend itself effectively against an evolving global terrorist threat, the United States will need flexible and adaptable policy instruments. In particular, previous distinctions between peacetime and wartime activities have less and less meaning in a world in which terrorists can strike anyplace at anytime.

Advisory and training activities have been particularly constrained by "peacetime" restrictions. Training deployments were typically limited to a few weeks or months; advisors were generally not allowed to accompany their units into combat; advisory organizations were underfunded and undermanned;[52] and career paths were often unclear or unattractive. In the new security environment, these activities need to be given the highest priority, the best personnel, and significant funding. Mobile training teams that visit host nations for a few weeks or months will continue to be useful. Experience shows, however, that a more-prolonged commitment is generally required to have lasting effects. The British use a more-successful model that embeds advisors in host-nation units for year-long tours. Recent U.S. experience in Iraq and Afghanistan has confirmed the great value of embedding advisors. Embedded advisors share hardships and risks with the host-nation forces over many months and, consequently, develop lasting relationships and credibility with the locals.

---

[51] In FY 2004, the top six recipients of military aid were Israel ($2.1 billion), Egypt ($1.3 billion), Afghanistan ($364 million), Jordan ($204 million), Colombia ($98 million), and Pakistan ($75 million). (See U.S. Department of State, Bureau of Resource Management, 2005, and U.S. Department of State, Bureau of Political-Military Affairs, 2005.)

[52] For example, the 6th Special Operations Squadron, the organization that provided U.S. Air Force combat aviation advisors, has only 109 personnel to cover the entire globe (Vick, Grissom, et al., 2006).

In the past, the U.S. training and advising focus has been on the host-nation land forces, and, as discussed previously, this likely will remain a mainstay of U.S. efforts. Air and naval operations were often neglected because the recipient nation lacked an air force or navy or because they were quite limited in their capabilities. Although the specific requirements will vary, U.S. advising and training should, as a general rule, help local forces become adept at joint and combined operations.[53]

U.S. combat aviation advisors can make important contributions even when the host lacks an air force. First, combat aviation advisors can help the host nation understand the contribution of air forces to joint operations and help determine the kinds of air capabilities (including unmanned systems) that are appropriate for their needs. This is not about building smaller versions of the U.S. Air Force but, rather, about identifying the capabilities that are the best match for the host nation's security needs. In many cases, that may mean procuring simple turboprop aircraft, helicopters, and UASs, rather than jet fighters.[54] Second, U.S. aviation advisors can help recipient nation ground force and joint commanders understand how U.S. or other friendly air forces might team with their ground forces to defeat internal or other threats. Combat aviation advisors can also help assisted nations develop the organizations, processes, and communication networks necessary to exploit the advantages that air power brings. Accomplishing these more-ambitious objectives will, however, require more Air Force per-

---

[53] A recent example of the great influence that air advising can have was the U.S. Air Force's training Philippine Air Force helicopter pilots in the use of night-vision goggles. Philippine ground force operations against insurgents were severely constrained by the lack of night medevac capability. Most operations were stopped by 1400 so that there would be little risk of afternoon casualties being stranded overnight. Once the Philippine helicopter pilots were able to fly night missions, it greatly boosted the morale of Philippine troops and resulted in a shift to 24-hour operations. The addition of this seemingly narrow skill fundamentally changed the nature of Philippine joint operations, significantly improving their combat effectiveness against insurgent and terrorist threats. (See McCarthy, 2004.)

[54] The value of relatively simple aircraft in counterinsurgency operations has been demonstrated in conflicts from Rhodesia to El Salvador. (See Corum and Johnson, 2003; Nesbit et al., 1999; and Bracamonte and Spencer, 1995.)

sonnel trained as combat aviation advisors and longer tours with the recipient nation's forces.

For littoral nations, naval advising, training, and equipping can be important as well. Naval forces have been active since 9/11 interdicting the movement of terrorists and weapons, but there are simply too many target vessels for the United States and other major navies to monitor. Local and regional coast guards are needed to monitor and board the thousands of small fishing and trading vessels. U.S. naval advisors are key to training these local navies and coast guards in interdiction, boarding, and related operations. Local forces using small patrol boats can be highly effective in these missions.

CHAPTER SIX

Potential Actions for DoD's Leadership

This report began by exploring the implications of three developments—terrorist groups with global reach, the proliferation of nuclear weapons, and the rise of China as a major power—that, collectively, spell the end of the post–Cold War era. We believe that these developments and the changes they have prompted in U.S. strategy will have profound and long-lasting effects on the nation and the ways in which it goes about protecting and advancing its interests worldwide. If U.S. armed forces are going to continue to serve the nation well, their capabilities, patterns of activity, and, in some cases, institutional cultures must adapt to these new circumstances.

The case set forth in this monograph calls for more highly differentiated roles among the services yet also for military operations characterized by increasing interdependence among the forces provided by each service. The report also points to the need for some new or greatly enhanced military capabilities. As the new leadership of DoD looks to set strategic direction for the armed forces, we recommend that it consider the following actions. While these recommendations are by no means comprehensive, they focus on bringing U.S. defense strategy, forces, and capabilities into better alignment with the demands of the nation's new strategy and with the types of challenges U.S. forces are likely to confront in the years to come.

Several of our suggested actions apply to DoD as a whole. They are aimed at generating greater breadth in needed capabilities while maintaining needed depth to contend with particular challenges. In a sense, these recommendations focus on reallocating risk to produce needed capabilities. In short, the recommendations form the essence of the "new division of labor" that we explore in this report. These include the following:

- **Recast U.S. defense strategy to incorporate "1-n-2-1" as its force sizing construct. Relieve the Army and Marine Corps of the requirement to provide forces for more than one major combat operation at a time.** Bringing stability to troubled nations, training and advising the forces of other countries, and conducting effective operations against insurgents and terrorists are important, complex, and politically charged missions. A greater level of effort is called for here if the United States and its allies are to make lasting progress against global terrorist threats. The accumulation of recent experience suggests that these missions cannot be done well by forces whose primary focus is large-scale combat. Changes in the nature of the threats regional adversaries pose will allow DoD to reduce the level of ground forces it plans to commit to major combat operations.
- **Complete the transition of the joint command structure.** Regional commanders need to remain focused on strategic matters, including achieving strategic victory in areas where U.S. forces are engaged. To allow them to do so, more and more-effective JTF headquarters are needed for running ongoing operations. Ongoing efforts in this regard at USJFCOM should be buttressed. Moreover, the joint division of labor among regional commands, global commands, and military services and supporting agencies should be clarified. The concept of a division of labor among users, managers, and providers may be useful in guiding this effort.
- **Complete the effort to realign U.S. global military posture and reevaluate that posture regularly.** The overseas posture of U.S. military forces and bases should directly reflect U.S. grand strategy. That is not the case today. Forces and bases will need to be realigned to support new democracies, counter terrorist and insurgent groups, deter and defeat regional adversaries, and dissuade military competition in Asia. Current plans for adjusting the global basing structure should be implemented and reevalu-

ated regularly to ensure that strategy and posture remain in proper alignment. Details are outlined in Chapter Three.

- **Increase investments in promising systems for surveillance and reconnaissance.** U.S. defense planners should aspire to put an end to the situation in which sensor systems and the means to interpret the information they acquire are chronically "low-density, high-demand" assets. And efforts should be made to accelerate the development of new systems better suited to finding such targets as mobile missiles, nuclear weapons, and small groups of armed combatants.

But realigning the defense strategy and reallocating risk alone will not provide the needed results. New partnerships need to be formed (and old ones need to be strengthened), new capabilities need to be developed, and new competencies need to be cultivated. These include:

- **Foster new and stronger partnerships among the military services to achieve greater strategic and operational depth and joint tactical proficiency.** Even as diversification among military services and agencies is required to support U.S. strategy, new interdependencies need to be forged. We view this as something akin to brokering a new set of partnerships among the military services. The process will be difficult, but in our judgment it is essential.
  - **Partnership 1: Develop and implement plans for air and land forces to train for and to conduct highly integrated operations.** To become more strategically deployable and agile on the battlefield, the Army is reducing its organic artillery and increasingly relying on air-delivered fires. Recent operations have demonstrated the potential of this concept, but it is far from established as a new way of war. Realistic air-ground exercises and training are rare, and procedures for controlling and integrating air operations and ground maneuver are outdated. The services need to see themselves as mutually enabling partners. Regular joint training, new fire control mechanisms

(including investments in new gear for tactical air controllers), and cultural changes will be necessary to realize the potential of the air-ground partnership.

— **Partnership 2: Foster much tighter links among air, naval, and space forces to create a more-durable, more-effective power-projection force.** Without better integrating the capabilities of America's air, naval, and space forces, the U.S. military runs the risk of not having an effective power-projection capability against adversaries with ballistic and cruise missiles, advanced air defenses, and perhaps nuclear weapons. Forging robust links will require more-routine training and the development of common command-and-control procedures and mechanisms.

— **Partnership 3: Promote a more-seamless integration between the Marine Corps and SOF.** Just as the Marine Corps could give SOF more depth by providing combined arms support for sensitive SOF missions, so too could the Marine Corps give SOF more reach by expanding the area and frequency of routine SOF missions and activities. These two branches have much in common, and they should exploit the exceptional qualities of both. This implies less focus on the Marine Corps' traditional amphibious missions and much more openness in the SOF community to cooperating with another military branch.

- **Pursue an aggressive effort to develop and produce more effective defenses against TBMs and cruise missiles.** These weapons, whether armed with accurate conventional warheads or nuclear weapons, pose grave obstacles to U.S. power-projection operations. Indeed, for the first time since the conclusion of the Cold War, the United States faces the prospect that its forces could be defeated or excluded from the fight. Large concentrations of troops and materiel within range of enemy missiles will be at great risk. And it may prove impossible to mount effective combat operations from even hardened fixed bases within range of these weapons. Because of the importance of protecting the civilian populations and infrastructures of allied nations, special emphasis should be placed on developing concepts for layered theater missile defenses that are effective over wide areas. Truly effective defenses will require the fielding of larger numbers of existing theater missile defense systems (e.g., the Theater High-Altitude Area Defense system and the U.S. Navy's SM-3) and one or more additional "layers" of active defense.

- **Greatly expand the capacity and competence of forces devoted to combat advisory and training missions.** New democracies and friendly nations threatened by insurgent and terrorist groups will look to the United States for assistance. It is neither desirable nor feasible to send U.S. land combat forces to fight other countries' insurgencies. Rather, the most effective means for DoD to counter terrorist and insurgent groups abroad is to train, equip, advise, and assist the forces of friendly governments. The United States already possesses first-rate combat advisors and trainers in all the services, but their numbers are small, resources are limited, and activities are greatly restricted. Substantial portions of the "regular" forces must contribute to this vital mission. Although the largest number of advisors will likely come from the Army and Marine Corps, the advisory capabilities of the U.S. Navy and Air Force need to expand as well. Expanded foreign area officer programs in the services are essential to develop the language and cultural understanding necessary to be effective advisors.

Finally, specific entities within DoD will need to adopt different approaches, develop new or refined capabilities, and cultivate new talents. But these changes will likely need outside intervention to "jump-start" the activity. We have highlighted the most important of these changes, including the following:

- **Direct the Army to explore creating distinct elements within its tactical structure. One element would specialize in conventional warfighting operations and the other would specialize in stability, support, and advisory operations.** Resource constraints and limitations on the ability of soldiers to master and maintain widely divergent skill sets make it impossible for the Army to fully prepare its entire tactical structure for both conventional warfighting and stability operations. By bifurcating its tactical structure, the Army would free the units assigned conventional missions to prepare more fully for warfighting operations and would free the units assigned to stability operations to prepare more fully for these difficult missions. The result would be that the Army as a whole would become more proficient at both.

- **Direct the Army to create doctrine and a professional military education curriculum that emphasize stability operations.** Current doctrine and curriculum focus on conventional warfighting to the near-exclusion of stability operations. This imbalance should be corrected by balancing capstone and operational-level doctrine equally between warfighting and stability operations. Tactical doctrine and training literature will likely need to be bifurcated by mission as well.

- **Direct the U.S. Air Force to reevaluate its concepts for large-scale power-projection operations, assessing in particular the implications for its mix of long- and short-range platforms.** The Air Force's planned investments in new combat aircraft implicitly reflect the belief that forces will be able to deploy forward and conduct high-tempo operations from air bases in the theater of conflict. Such assumptions seem increasingly untenable. A platform mix that emphasized long-range platforms for surveillance and strike would provide commanders more options for basing aircraft in locales less threatened by attack from enemy missiles. It would also provide more "battle space," allowing defensive systems more opportunities to engage incoming missiles. Longer-range platforms would also be better suited to providing enduring, responsive information and fire support to joint forces on battlefields where enemy forces are less likely to be massed and more likely to be encountered episodically.

- **Help rebuild the nation's intelligence system—and by implication DoD's intelligence capabilities—by focusing first and foremost on the human dimension.** New sensors, platforms, and technologies are vital to answering the challenges of the future security environment—and we believe that a thorough reassessment of investment priorities is needed. However, above all, enabling decisionmakers at the tactical, operational, and strategic levels demands properly trained and experienced people throughout the collection, assessment, and dissemination chain. Especially within the four military services, more people are needed with the skills to understand the political and social dynamics in troubled regions. And institutional incentives must be put in place to create satisfying career paths that encourage and reward professionalism.

- **Direct U.S. air forces to train more frequently with U.S. SOF and the ground forces of friendly nations.** In most cases, U.S. involvement in counterinsurgency operations will be limited to advising, equipping, and training. Where the threat is particularly great or host-nation capabilities are limited, the United States may want to provide direct operational support. Because a large or highly visible presence can undermine the credibility of the government the United States seeks to support, direct support must have a minimal footprint. U.S. air forces can provide critical surveillance, strike, and lift support in low-key ways, flying from remote bases or even from outside the assisted country. When combined with competent local ground forces, U.S. air forces can be extremely effective against insurgents. To be effective working with local forces, selected elements from U.S. air forces will need to train with U.S. SOF, U.S. Air Force terminal attack controllers, and allied ground forces on a regular basis.

Finally, while striving to fix what is broken, DoD should be careful not to break what is fixed. The U.S. armed forces are the most powerful and successful in the world, perhaps in history. Their dominance of the conventional "force on force" battlefield is so overwhelming that it has, among other things, rendered a whole class of historically troubling scenarios—massed cross-border aggression by large, armored forces—largely obsolete. Maintaining the capabilities that have created this situation is critically important. Continued, selective investment in the areas in which the United States currently enjoys "overmatch" will be needed alongside the new initiatives required to address the nation's emerging security problems.

Bibliography

Albright, Madeline, *Madame Secretary*, New York: Miramax Books, 2003.

Bacevich, Andrew J., *The New American Militarism: How Americans are Seduced by War*, New York: Oxford University Press, 2005.

Barnett, Thomas P. M., *The Pentagon's New Map*, New York: G.P. Putnam's Sons, 2004.

Bernstein, Richard, and R. H. Munro, *The Coming Conflict with China*, New York: Vintage, 1998.

Bracamonte, Jose Angel Moroni, and David E. Spencer, *Strategy and Tactics of the Salvadoran FMLN Guerrillas: Last Battle of the Cold War, Blueprint for Future Conflicts*, New York: Praeger Publishers, 1995.

Brozenick, Norman J., *Another Way to Fight: Combat Aviation Advisory Operations*, Maxwell Air Force Base, Ala.: Air University, 2002.

Bush, George [H. W.], and Brent Scowcroft, *A World Transformed*, New York: Alfred A. Knopf, Inc., 1998.

Bush, George W., "Second Inaugural Address," Washington, D.C., January 20, 2005.

Bush, George W., statement at joint press conference with Vladimir Putin, Bratislava, Slovak Republic, February 24, 2005.

Central Intelligence Agency, *The World Factbook 2004*, Washington, D.C.: 2004. Current version as of April 21, 2006:
http://www.cia.gov/cia/publications/factbook/index.html

Chicago Council on Foreign Relations, *Global Views 2004: American Public Opinion and Foreign Policy,* Chicago, Ill., 2004.

Childress, Michael, *The Effectiveness of U.S. Training Efforts in Internal Defense and Development: The Cases of El Salvador and Honduras*, Santa Monica, Calif.: RAND Corporation, MR-250-USDP, 1995. As of January 3, 2007:
http://www.rand.org/pubs/monograph_reports/MR250/

Cliff, Roger, Mark Burles, Michael S. Chase, Derek Eaton, and Kevin L. Pollpeter, *Entering the Dragon's Lair: Chinese Antiaccess Strategies and Their Implications for the United States*, Santa Monica, Calif.: RAND Corporation, 2007.

Corum, James S., and Wray R. Johnson, *Airpower in Small Wars: Fighting Insurgents and Terrorists,* Lawrence, Kan.: University of Kansas Press, 2003.

Cragin, Kim, and S. A. Daly, *The Dynamic Terrorist Threat: An Assessment of Group Motivations and Capabilities in a Changing World*, Santa Monica, Calif.: RAND Corporation, MR-1782-AF, 2004. As of January 3, 2007: http://www.rand.org/pubs/monograph_reports/MR1782/

Crane, Keith, Roger Cliff, Evan Medeiros, James C. Mulvenon, and William H. Overholt, *Modernizing China's Military: Opportunities and Constraints*, Santa Monica, Calif.: RAND Corporation, MG-260-AF, 2005. As of January 3, 2007: http://www.rand.org/pubs/monographs/MG260-1/

Defense Security Cooperation Agency, "Frequently Asked Questions (FAQs)," Web page, last revised May 23, 2005. As of April 21, 2006: http://www.dsca.mil/PressReleases/faq.htm

Diel, Jackson, "Battle for Egypt's Future," *Washington Post*, April 25, 2005, p. A19.

Dobbins, James, John McGinn, Keith Crane, Seth Jones, Rollie Lal, Andrew Rathmell, and Anga Timilsina, *America's Role in Nation-Building: From Germany to Iraq*, Santa Monica, Calif.: RAND Corporation, MR-1753-RC, 2003. As of January 3, 2007: http://www.rand.org/pubs/monograph_reports/MR1753/

DoD—*See* U.S. Department of Defense.

"Egypt Criticizes U.S. 'Democracy' Initiative, Jordan, Qatar, Israel Welcome," *IslamOnline*, December 13, 2004. As of April 21, 2006: http://www.islamonline.net/English/News/2002-12/13/article09.shtml

Eisenhower, Dwight D., "First Inaugural Address," Washington, D.C., January 20, 1953.

Franks, Tommy, *American Soldier*, New York: HarperCollins Inc., 2004.

Freedman, Lawrence, "Order and Disorder in the New World," *Foreign Affairs,* Vol. 71, No. 1, Winter 1991/1992.

Gordon, John, and David Orletsky, "Moving Rapidly to the Fight," in Lynn E. Davis and Jeremy Shapiro, eds., *The U.S. Army and the New National Security Strategy*, Santa Monica, Calif.: RAND Corporation, MR-1657-A, 2003. As of January 3, 2007: http://www.rand.org/pubs/monograph_reports/MR1657/

Graham, Bradley, and Glenn Kessler, "N. Korea Nuclear Advance is Cited," *Washington Post*, April 29, 2005, p. 1.

Headquarters Department of the Army, "Stability Operations and Support Operations," Washington, D.C., FM 3-07, 2003.

Headquarters Department of the Army, "The 2005 Army Modernization Plan," Washington, D.C., February 2005.

Headquarters U.S. Marine Corps, "Marine Corps Order 3120.9B. Subject: Policy for Marine Expeditionary Unit (Special Operations Capable) (MEU [SOC])," Washington, D.C., September 25, 2001.

Hoffman, Bruce, "Al Qaeda, Trends in Terrorism, and Future Potentialities: An Assessment," Santa Monica, Calif.: RAND Corporation, P-8078, 2003. As of January 3, 2007:
http://www.rand.org/pubs/papers/P8078/

———, "Insurgency and Counterinsurgency in Iraq," Santa Monica, Calif.: RAND Corporation, OP-127-IPC/CMEPP, 2004. As of January 3, 2007:
http://www.rand.org/pubs/occasional_papers/OP127/

Holley, David, "Russia, China Team Up to Assail U.S. Foreign Policy," *Los Angeles Times*, July 2, 2005, p. A9.

Hosmer, Stephen, *The Army's Role in Counterinsurgency and Insurgency*, Santa Monica, Calif.: RAND Corporation, R-3947-A, 1992. As of January 3, 2007:
http://www.rand.org/pubs/reports/R3947/

Hosmer, Stephen T., *Operations Against Enemy Leaders*, Santa Monica, Calif.: RAND Corporation, MR-1385-AF, 2001. As of January 3, 2007:
http://www.rand.org/pubs/monograph_reports/MR1385/

Hyland, William G., "America's New Course," *Foreign Affairs*, Vol. 21, No. 2, Spring 1990, pp. 1–12.

Information Office of the State Council of the People's Republic of China, *The Human Rights Record of the United States in 2004*, March 3, 2005.

Joes, Anthony James, *Resisting Rebellion: The History and Politics of Counterinsurgency*, Lexington, Ky.: The University Press of Kentucky, 2004.

Johnson, David E., *Learning Large Lessons: The Evolving Roles of Ground Power and Air Power in the Post–Cold War Era*, Santa Monica, Calif.: RAND Corporation, MG-405-1-AF, 2007.

Kennedy, John F., "Inaugural Address," Washington, D.C., January 20, 1961.

Kerry, John, Remarks at Temple University, Philadelphia, Pa., September 24, 2004.

Khalilzad, Zalmay, David T. Orletsky, Jonathan D. Pollack, Kevin L. Pollpeter, Angel Rabasa, David A. Shlapak, Abram N. Shulsky, and Ashley J. Tellis, *The United States and Asia: Toward a New U.S. Strategy and Force Posture*,

Santa Monica, Calif.: RAND Corporation, MR-1315-AF, 2001. As of January 3, 2007:
http://www.rand.org/pubs/monograph_reports/MR1315/

Killingsworth, Paul S., Lionel Galway, Eiichi Kamiya, Brian Nichiporuk, Timothy L. Ramey, Robert S. Tripp, and James C. Wendt, *Flexbasing: Achieving Global Presence for Expeditionary Aerospace Forces*, Santa Monica, Calif.: RAND Corporation, MR-1113-AF, 2000. As of January 3, 2007:
http://www.rand.org/pubs/monograph_reports/MR1113/

Krauthammer, Charles, "The Unipolar Moment," *Foreign Affairs,* Vol. 70, No. 1, Winter 1990/1991.

Ma, Jason, "Marine Corps to Support U.S. SOCOM in Training Foreign Militaries," *Inside the Navy*, April 25, 2005, p. 4.

McCarthy, Thomas, *National Security for the 21st Century: The Air Force and Foreign Internal Defense,* master's thesis, Maxwell Air Force Base, Ala.: School for Advanced Air and Space Studies, 2004.

Metz, Steven, and Raymond Millen, *Insurgency and Counterinsurgency in the 21st Century: Reconceptualizing Threat and Response*, Carlisle Barracks, Pa.: U.S. Army Strategic Studies Institute, 2004.

Mulvenon, James C., and R. H. Yang, *The People's Liberation Army in the Information Age*, Santa Monica, Calif.: RAND Corporation, CF-145-CAPP/AF, 1999. As of January 3, 2007:
http://www.rand.org/pubs/conf_proceedings/CF145/

Nardulli, Bruce, "The U.S. Army and the Offensive War on Terrorism," in Lynn E. Davis and Jeremy Shapiro, eds., *The U.S. Army and the New National Security Strategy*, Santa Monica, Calif.: RAND Corporation, MR-1657-A, 2003. As of January 3, 2007:
http://www.rand.org/pubs/monograph_reports/MR1657/

Nathan, Andrew J., and R. S. Ross, *The Great Wall and the Empty Fortress*, New York: Norton, 1998.

"Navy to Base First Littoral Combat Ship in San Diego," *Navy Newsstand,* December 3, 2005. As of April 21, 2006:
http://www.news.navy.mil/search/display.asp?story_id=21247

Nesbit, Roy Conyers, et al., *Britain's Rebel Air Force: The War for Rhodesia 1965–1980,* London: Grub Street Publishing, 1999.

Nitze, Paul H., "America: Honest Broker," *Foreign Affairs*, Vol. 69, No. 4, Fall 1990, pp. 1–14.

Ochmanek, David, *Military Operations Against Terrorist Groups Abroad: Implications for the United States Air Force*, Santa Monica, Calif.: RAND Corporation, MR-1738-AF, 2003. As of January 3, 2007:
http://www.rand.org/pubs/monograph_reports/MR1738/

Pirnie, Bruce R., Alan Vick, Adam Grissom, Karl P. Mueller, and David T. Orletsky, *Beyond Close Air Support: Forging a New Air-Ground Partnership,* Santa Monica, Calif.: RAND Corporation, MG-301-AF, 2005. As of January 3, 2007: http://www.rand.org/pubs/monographs/MG301/

Putin, Vladimir, statement at joint press conference with George W. Bush, Bratislava, Slovak Republic, February 24, 2005.

Rabasa, Angel M., Cheryl Benard, Peter Chalk, C. Christine Fair, Theodore Karasik, Rollie Lal, Ian Lesser, and David Thaler, *The Muslim World After 9/11,* Santa Monica, Calif.: RAND Corporation, MG-246-AF, 2004. As of January 3, 2007: http://www.rand.org/pubs/monographs/MG246/

Rabasa, Angel M., Peter Chalk, R. Kim Cragin, Sara A. Daly, Heather S. Gregg, Theodore W. Karasik, Kevin A. O'Brien, and William Rosenau, *Beyond al-Qaeda: Part 1, the Global Jihadist Movement,* Santa Monica, Calif.: RAND Corporation, MG-429-AF, 2006. As of January 3, 2007: http://www.rand.org/pubs/monographs/MG429/

Roosevelt, Franklin D., "The 'Four Freedoms,'" speech delivered to the Congress of the United States, Washington, D.C., January 6, 1941.

Schoomaker, Peter J., and Francis K. Harvey, "The Army 2005 Posture Statement," Washington, D.C.: Headquarters Department of the Army, February 6, 2005.

Second Marine Expeditionary Force, "Nasiriyah," After Action Report, 2003.

Shambaugh, David, *Modernizing China's Military: Progress, Problems, and Prospects,* Berkeley, Calif.: University of California, 2004.

Sharansky, Natan, *The Case for Democracy: The Power of Freedom to Overcome Tyranny and Terror,* New York: Public Affairs, 2004.

Shim, Jae-yun, "President Opposes Role for USFK in Regional Conflict," *Korea Times,* March 8, 2005.

Shlapak, David A., *Shaping the Future Air Force,* Santa Monica, Calif.: RAND Corporation, TR-322-AF, 2006.

Shlapak, David A., David Orletsky, and Barry A. Wilson, *Dire Strait?: Military Aspects of the China-Taiwan Confrontation and Options for U.S. Policy,* Santa Monica, Calif.: RAND Corporation, MR-1217-SRF, 2000. As of January 3, 2007: http://www.rand.org/pubs/monograph_reports/MR1217/

Shlapak, David A., John Stillion, Olga Oliker, and Tanya Charlick-Paley, *A Global Access Strategy for the U.S. Air Force,* Santa Monica, Calif.: RAND Corporation, MR-1216-AF, 2002. As of January 3, 2007: http://www.rand.org/pubs/monograph_reports/MR1216/

Shlapak, David A., and Alan Vick, *Check Six Begins on the Ground: Responding to the Evolving Ground Threat to U.S. Air Force Bases*, Santa Monica, Calif.: RAND Corporation, MR-606-AF, 1995.

"Should the West Always Be Worried if Islamists Win Elections?" *The Economist*, April 28, 2005.

Sorensen, Theodore, "Rethinking National Security," *Foreign Affairs*, Vol. 69, No. 3, Summer 1990, pp. 131–146.

Stillion, John, and David T. Orletsky, *Airbase Vulnerability to Conventional Cruise-Missile and Ballistic-Missile Attacks: Technology, Scenarios, and U.S. Air Force Responses*, Santa Monica, Calif.: RAND Corporation, MR-1028-AF, 1999. As of January 3, 2007:
http://www.rand.org/pubs/monograph_reports/MR1028/

Tirpak, J. A., "The New Way of Electron War," *Air Force*, Vol. 87, No. 12, December 2004. As of April 24, 2006:
http://www.afa.org/magazine/dec2004/1204electron.html

U.S. Army, *On Point: The United States Army in Operation Iraqi Freedom*, 2003.

———, "Building Army Capabilities," draft Army briefing for POTUS, January 28, 2004. As of 2005:
http://www.comw.org/qdr/fulltext/0401armstructbrief.ppt+%22Building+Army+Capabilities%22&hl=en

———, *Posture Statement 2005*, February 6, 2005. As of April 26, 2006:
http://www.army.mil/aps/05/index.html

U.S. Army Training and Doctrine Command, *Prepare the Army for War: A Historical Overview of the Army Training and Doctrine Command 1973–1998*, Hampton, Va., 1999.

U.S. Department of Defense, *Report on the Bottom-Up Review*, Washington, D.C., 1993.

———, *Quadrennial Defense Review Report*, Washington, D.C., September 30, 2001.

———, *Department of Defense Reserve Component Employment Study 2005*, Washington, D.C.: 2005a.

———, *Military Support for Stability, Security, Transition, and Reconstruction Operations*, Washington, D.C., DoD Directive 3000.05, November 2005b.

———, *Quadrennial Defense Review Report*, Washington, D.C., February 6, 2006.

U.S. Department of Defense, Security Cooperation Agency, *Frequently Asked Questions*, Washington, D.C., 2005. As of April 21, 2006:
http://www.dsca.mil/pressreleases/faq.htm

U.S. Department of Defense and U.S. Department of State, *Foreign Military Training and DoD Engagement Activities of Interest*, 2002–2004. As of January 3, 2007:
http://www.state.gov/t/pm/rls/rpt/fmtrpt/

U.S. Department of State, Bureau of Political-Military Affairs, "International Military Education and Training Account Summaries," Web page, 2005. As of April 24, 2006:
http://www.state.gov/t/pm/ppa/sat/c14562.htm

U.S. Department of State, Bureau of Resource Management, "International Affairs Budget," Web page, 2005. Current version as of April 24, 2006:
http://www.state.gov/m/rm/c6112.htm

U.S. Department of the Navy, *Vision, Presence, Power: A Program Guide to the U.S. Navy*, Washington, D.C., 2004.

———, *Navy's 3/1 Strategy: A Strategy for a Navy that is Dominant, Relevant and Affordable*, draft, Washington, D.C., February 2006.

U.S. European Command, "Georgia Train and Equip Program Fact Sheet," Vaihingen, Germany, n.d. (circa 2003).

Vick, Alan, Richard Moore, Bruce Pirnie, and John Stillion, *Aerospace Operations Against Elusive Ground Targets*, Santa Monica, Calif.: RAND Corporation, MR-1398-AF, 2001. As of January 3, 2007:
http://www.rand.org/pubs/monograph_reports/MR1398/

Vick, Alan, David Orletsky, Bruce Pirnie, and Seth Jones, *The Stryker Brigade Combat Team: Rethinking Responsiveness and Assessing Deployment Options*, Santa Monica, Calif.: RAND Corporation, MR-1606-AF, 2002. As of January 3, 2007:
http://www.rand.org/pubs/monograph_reports/MR1606/

Vick, Alan J., Adam Grissom, William Rosenau, Beth Grill, and Karl P. Mueller, *Air Power in the New Counterinsurgency Era: The Strategic Importance of USAF Advisory and Assistance Missions*, Santa Monica, Calif.: RAND Corporation, MG-509-AF, 2006. As of January 3, 2007:
http://www.rand.org/pubs/monographs/MG509/

Weiner, Tim, "An Army Program to Build a High-Tech Force Hits Cost Snags," *New York Times*, March 28, 2005, p. 1.

White House, "George Washington," Web page, undated. As of April 21, 2006:
http://www.whitehouse.gov/history/presidents/gw1.html

———, *The National Security Strategy of the United States of America*, Washington, D.C., August 1991.

———, *A National Security Strategy of Engagement and Enlargement*, Washington, D.C., July 1994.

————, *National Strategy for Combating Terrorism*, Washington, D.C., February 2003.

Whittle, Richard, "Division Reorganized for Return Trip: Emphasis Shifted to Brigades as Agile, Main Fighting Formations," *Dallas Morning News*, April 30, 2005.

Wilson, John B., *Maneuver and Firepower: The Evolution of Divisions and Separate Brigades*, Washington, D.C.: U.S. Army Center for Military History, 1998.

Wilson, Peter A., John Gordon, and David E. Johnson, "An Alternative Future Force: Building a Better Army," *Parameters*, Winter 2003/2004, pp. 19–39.

Wilson, Woodrow, "Fourteen Points," speech delivered to the Joint Session of Congress, Washington, D.C., January 8, 1918.

Wright, Robin, and Josh White, "U.S. Moves to Preserve Iraq Coalition," *Washington Post*, February 25, 2005, p. A1.

Zakaria, Fareed, *The Future of Freedom: Illiberal Democracy at Home and Abroad*, New York: W.W. Norton & Company, 2003.